"Pat Stokes is a highly organized thinker undertaking the Herculean task of codifying the chaos called 'Creativity.' (Tantamount to holding a pint of water in your hand.) Densely packed with convincing examples, her concept that problem solving and obstacles propel creativity is fed to us step-by-step until we understand how we got where we are."

—*Les Richter*
Former Creative Director of Ted Bates, and Professional Potter

"Stokes provides language in which to frame artistic experience, and mine it more profitably. This book is a very useful tool in emphasizing the importance of problem posing in conjunction with problem-solving skills, and can enrich approaches to creative problem solving."

—*Adelheid Mers*
Artist and Instructor at the Art Institute of Chicago

"In writing about constraints and setting goals and bringing those goals to successful conclusions or further goal setting, Dr. Stokes has produced a fascinating book giving us insights into the creative process. As a painter/printmaker, much of this hits home, and the book has me reviewing my own personal experiences."

—*Richard Pantell*
Artist and Instructor at the Art Students League
New York City

"Using case studies of individuals working in various aspects of the arts, Stokes offers well-informed and insightful analysis of the complex phenomenon we call creativity. This survey is a piece of research and exploration that is thorough and engaging."

—*John (Andy) Hoogenboom*
Printer, Sculptor, and Photographer

About the Author

Pat Stokes teaches and conducts research at Barnard College, Columbia University, where she is an adjunct professor of psychology. However, her expertise on creativity is hands-on. Prior to becoming a psychologist, she painted at Pratt, wrote advertising copy at J. Walter Thompson, and became a creative group head at Ted Bates & Co. Her approach is that of a practitioner, applying a constraint-based strategy (acquired in art and advertising) to analyze the careers of renowned creators, to interview current creators, and to help future creators understand their own development.

CREATIVITY
FROM CONSTRAINTS

The Psychology of Breakthrough

Patricia D. Stokes, PhD

SPRINGER PUBLISHING COMPANY

Springer Publishing Company, Inc.
11 West 42nd Street
New York, NY 10036

Acquisitions Editor: Lauren Dockett
Production Editor: Betsy Day
Cover design by Mimi Flow

06 07 08 09 10 / 5 4 3 2 1

Library of Congress Cataloging-in-Publication Data

Stokes, Patricia D.
   Creativity from constraints : the psychology of breakthrough / Patricia D. Stokes.— 1st ed.
       p. cm.
   "Written for psychologists who study creativity and problem solving, skill acquisition and expertise, development and education, this book is also of practical use to researchers and clinicians, the success of whose designs—experimental and clinical—depends on the creative choice of constraints. Learn about: - Strategic and structural constraints - Constraints as creative tools - Application of constraints to clinical experimentation"—Provided by the publisher.
   Includes bibliographical references and index.
   ISBN 0-8261-7845-6 (pbk.)
   1. Creative ability. 2. Creation (Literary, artistic, etc.)
3. Problem solving. I. Title.

BF408.S78 2005
153.3'5—dc22

2005018663

Printed in the United States of America by Kase Printing.

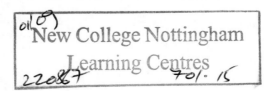

To my husband, Ron Romano,
the most creative person I know.

Contents

Preface

ART SCHOOL AND ADVERTISING

This book grew out of things I learned in art school and in advertising, things which I only understood when I became a psychologist.

Psychology obviously is my second career. I would say teaching too except that when I was a group head, I taught cub copy writers. That career, the first one, was in advertising. I went to Pratt. I worked at J. Walter Thompson, Ted Bates, Jordan Case McGrath. I wrote on national accounts, primarily on package goods—things that come in packages and are sold on shelves. I worked on food (Wonder Bread, Good Seasons), toiletries (Arrid, Ponds), cosmetics (Avon, Maybelline, Helena Rubenstein).

It was terrific. I even got to work in Tokyo for three years. It was terrific for a long time, and then something terrible happened—I got bored. In a creative business, where I was successful, I got bored. (We'll get back to boredom as a catalyst).

To get un-bored, I went to back to school, to Columbia, for a PhD. I always wanted to be a doctor, a certified expert. Why psychology? I worked in the "creative department," where success meant solving the same problem, selling the same product, over and over in different ways. Psychologists studied creativity. I read a lot of what psychologists wrote. Much of it was about traits, talent, genius, stuff you have or don't have: not very useful in an advertising agency. The parts that were more pragmatic— training, steps, strategies—never came close to what goes on in a professional school like Pratt or an advertising agency like Bates. Let me tell you something about art school and advertising:

At Pratt, my instructor for life drawing was a sculptor named Calvin Albert. The class lasted three hours. Half that time we drew to solve the problem he set that day; the other half, we could draw any way we liked. One drawing problem I remember was "Pretend that the top half of the model's body is in shadow, and that the light gets harsher as you go from one sketch to the next." We had to imagine the shadow and its shifting source, put in shadow shapes where there were none, adjust the values. What fascinated me was that the drawings done to Albert's specifications were always more interesting, more creative, more compelling, than those we composed when left to our own devices.

At Thompson and Bates, television spots were increasingly original, pointed, and (most importantly) persuasive when written to an exactly worded promise. The promise was the single most important benefit the product could deliver to its consumer. Coming up with the promise was the big problem. Bates called these promises USPs, unique selling propositions. (We'll cover lots of these in chapter 7.)

Why do USPs work? You don't get writer's block when you have something to say. More specific promises make for easier execution. Think about selling a suntan lotion. What's the promise? A tan? All suntan lotions can promise that. A dark, sexy tan? Ban de Soléil owns that one. How about a "baby oil tan without baby oil burn"? That's the promise I wrote for Sea and Ski when I worked at Bates.

CONSTRAINTS AND THE CREATIVITY PROBLEM

What do these examples from art school and advertising have in common? They use constraints to promote creativity. (They exclude, of course, constraints that promote conformity, e.g., copy or calculate correctly.) As we'll see in chapters 4 and 7, the results in art and advertising are the same: The more constrained the solution paths, the more variable, the more creative, the problem solvers.

"But," someone always asks, "what about artistic freedom"? Free to do anything, most of us do what's worked best, what has succeeded most often in the past. This is, in fact, the definition of an operant: a behavior that increases in frequency because it has been successful. Successful solutions are reliable, not surprising; predictable, not novel; already accepted, not creative. Highly rewarded for their expertise, experts get stuck in successful solutions—that's why they get bored. So, the answer to the "freedom" question is this: Being completely free hinders solving what I call the creativity problem.

The creativity problem is *strategic* and *structural*. It involves selecting (the strategy part) paired constraints (the structure part) that preclude reliable, successful responses and promote novel, surprising ones. Constraints for creativity involve substitutions: new for old, exploratory for tried-and-true. However, "new" and "old" alone won't do—each one must be *specified*.

For example, at the start of the Impressionist movement, Monet's constraints *precluded* dark-light contrasts which, by extension, precluded both the illusion of depth and sharply outlined shapes (specific old ways of producing representational paintings). They simultaneously *promoted* contrasting closely-valued colors, which, in turn, promoted flat patterns with soft-edged shapes that shared brushstrokes and colors (specific new ways). Monet didn't come up with those constraints arbitrarily. They were *strategically chosen* to realize his new goal criterion—showing how light breaks up on surfaces.

Identifying Monet's constraint path allows us to re-create the *structure* of his solution. How does light break up on things? In "Regatta at Sainte-Addresse" (1867), in bright, clear, contrasting hues, in cream-colored sails casting Prussian blue shadows on a teal green sea.

PSYCHOLOGY

In chapter 4, a case study considers Monet's development constraint by constraint. Why so carefully? To answer a question that I keep finding new answers to: *What can we learn from Monet?* If we understand how Monet used constraints, we'll have learned some important things about solving the creativity problem. Case studies in other chapters ask the Monet question (*What can we learn from?*) of creators in different domains—art, advertising, architecture, fashion, literature, and music. Most are famous. A conversation with a practicing, proficient, but not-well-known person is included for each domain. This is purposeful. Its purpose is to demonstrate that, at all levels of expertise and influence, paired constraints are the most used and the most useful ways to solve the creativity problem. Interestingly, all my interviewees found it easy—and also revealing—to think and talk about their work in terms of constraints.

Before the case studies and conversations, problem solving, the creativity problem (chapter 1), and the kinds of constraints that structure it (chapter 2) are covered. One constraint provides the first choruses that novices master and one which experts improvise. "First chorus" is a musical term for an initially played melody that provides the notes, chords, and keys used in the variations or improvisations that follow. For example, Mozart used the traditional melody *Twinkle, Twinkle, Little Star* as the basis for 12 variations. First choruses in other domains also supply components to be recombined and changed. In painting Seurat and Signac used Monet's mosaic-shaped brush strokes as a first chorus for developing the dots of pure color that characterize Pointillism.

The next-to-last chapter details the constraint-driven developmental path from child to creator; the last serves as a recap. There are also Appendices. They include shorter sections called *Working With Constraints,* exercises that have helped students (mine at Columbia, a friend's at the School of the Art Institute in Chicago) recognize, choose, and practice using constraints. Two are domain-specific (e.g., *Writing in a different voice*). One is more general *(Charting your own constraints)* and is meant for experts of all kinds.

A caveat: despite the exercises, this is not meant to be a "self-help" book. There are no six or seven easy steps to jump-start creativity. There are only two and they're both difficult. The first step is mastering the constraints that define a domain (its first choruses); the second is devising novel constraints that expand it.

CHAPTER 1

The Creativity Problem

What can we learn from Braque? What can we learn from Picasso? What can we learn from Cubism?

Creativity happens when someone does something *new* that is also useful or generative or influential (Csikszentmihalyi, 1996; Simonton, 1999). *Useful* means that the new thing solves a problem. (A doodle becomes the solution for a composition problem in a design class.) *Generative* means that the new thing leads to other ideas or things. (A solution suggests further developments or variations or facilitates solving the next problem.) *Influential* means that the new thing changes the way people look at, or listen to, or think about, or do, things like it. (Automatic writing, a kind of doodling invented by the Surrealists, was adapted by the Abstract Expressionists.)

This chapter's example of influential creativity comes from early in the 20th century. The creators were collaborators, a pair of painters—Georges Braque and Pablo Picasso. Between 1906 and 1914, Braque and Picasso developed a novel way to represent the world (Cooper, 1971; Rubin, 1989). Their new something, called Cubism, changed how some people (critics, dealers, collectors) looked at and thought about representational painting, and it changed how some other people (artists) painted. In short, our collaborators expanded their domain for all subsequent representational paintings (i.e., other things like it).

CUBISM: LEARNING FROM ART HISTORY

In 1906, when Braque and Picasso began to paint together, accepted representational painting styles shared two related criteria that Cubism shattered. Artists painted *what they saw,* from a *single point of view.* Imagine three landscapes: the first by Manet, with outlined, simple, clearly modeled shapes; the second by Monet, with pale, muted blues, purples, and pinks reflected in water; the third by Matisse, with bright, saturated hues applied in a decorative pattern. The paintings differ radically in palette, brush stroke, and composition, but each shows what the artist saw. Manet, the naturalist, saw how objects look. Monet, the Impressionist, saw how light looks. Matisse, the Fauvist, saw how pure, undiluted color looks. All three looked into spaces of varying depth, but always straight ahead.

What Braque and Picasso attempted to paint was *what they knew,* from *multiple viewpoints,* and wound up with little, if any, depth.

How could they "see" a compote of fruit from the top and the side at the same time? It's very difficult, but we can try to approximate it by starting with separate views and then combining them. The left panel in Figure 1.1 shows a compote of fruit from the side. The right panel shows it on top of a checkered tablecloth, from above. What would be an acceptable combination? If we look closely at a Braque or Picasso, the answer seems to be, one with an overall pattern, a rhythm to move the eye around the surface of the painting. Exaggerating values (light and dark contrasts) helps this happen.

Figure 1.2 shows one possible combination. Braque it's not, but it does approximate a Cubist composition. We're looking down at the inside

FIGURE 1.1. Two views of a fruit compote.

FIGURE 1.2. Combining the two drawings from Figure 1.1.

of the bowl and straight ahead at its foot. The checkered cloth is now inside the bowl and the whole picture has picked up its black-and-white pattern.

This exercise merely suggests the enormity of the problem Braque and Picasso were solving. If it was difficult for Braque and Picasso to "see" in the new Cubist way, imagine how hard it was for their audience. As you would expect, when they first showed their new paintings, most people thought they were plain crazy. To persist, their work had to be *generative*—that is, it had to provide a basis from which Braque and Picasso developed variations in their new Cubist style. To change the judgment from crazy to creative, the work had to be *influential*, and in two ways. One was changing how other artists saw and represented the world. The other was changing how dealers, critics, and collectors saw representational painting.

Cubism was creative according to all three of our definition's criteria. It was *useful* in solving the problem posed by Picasso and Braque. It was *generative* in leading to variations on that solution. It was *influential* in changing the way others saw, and made, paintings.

CUBISM: LEARNING FROM PSYCHOLOGY

Creating Cubism was a problem that took Braque and Picasso eight years (1906–1914) to solve. A partial answer to questions like "Why so long?" and "Why so difficult?" comes from a short primer on problem-solving.

Well- and Ill-Structured Problems

A problem is classified as well- or ill-structured depending on the information provided for its solution (Newell & Simon, 1972; Reitman, 1965; Simon, 1973; Voss & Post, 1988). Based on the information and on the solver's expertise, a problem space—a representation of the problem—is constructed. A problem space has an initial and a goal state, a set of operators (condition-action rules of the form, "If this condition, then this action") that are applied sequentially to move from the initial to the goal state, and a criterion for knowing when the goal is reached. Constraints help structure the solution path by limiting (precluding) and directing (promoting) search in a problem space.

In a *well-structured problem*, everything in the problem space is specified. In the domain of representational painting, painting-by-number is a well-structured problem. The initial state is a canvas with a numbered cartoon drawing printed on it. The canvas comes with a set of numbered paints. The goal criterion is matching the picture on the cover of the paint-by-number set. There is one operator, which is applied recursively: "If the number on the cartoon is N, fill the space with the paint marked N."

Table 1.1 illustrates the problem space for paint-by-number. Notice that in this and all well-structured problems there is little search and, importantly, a single correct goal state. This precludes creativity; creativity is only possible with ill-structured problems.

An *ill-structured problem* is incompletely specified. What is left out? The operators or the order in which they are applied may be unknown. More critical to creativity, there could be no clear goal criterion, which was the case with Cubism and was also why it took so long to develop as an art form.

TABLE 1.1. Problem Space for Paint-by-Number Problem

Initial State
    Canvas with numbered cartoon.
    Numbered set of paints.

Operators
    1. If section is numbered "1," fill with paint numbered "1."
    2. If section is numbered "2," fill with paint numbered "2."
    3. Continue until all sections are filled.

Goal State
    Match picture on cover of paint-by-number set.

The initial state for Braque and Picasso was representational painting. In 1906, this included Monet's Impressionism, Matisse's Fauvism, and more traditional styles using *chiaroscuro,* dark-light contrasts that produced a convincing illusion of depth. The operators and the goal criterion evolved between 1906 and 1914. Table 1.2 oversimplifies the search space by including only three of these operations.

My attempt at a Cubist composition (Figure 1.2) was produced using the three operators from Figure 1.1: (1) The compote and its contents are fractured and shown from several viewpoints; (2) the hues are limited to black and white, and their values to very light and very dark; (3) the recombined parts are arranged in a checkerboard pattern.

The Creativity Problem: Strategy and Structure

The defining characteristics of what I call the creativity problem are three. First and obviously, it is initially ill-structured. Second, its solution depends on strategic specification of paired constraints. The specification is *strategic* because it is determined by the goal criterion. Third, the selected constraints *structure* the problem space to preclude (or limit search among) familiar, reliable responses and promote (or direct search among) novel, surprising ones. As we shall see, studying the development of constraint pairs in a particular work (or better, a body of work) can *re-create* its solution path.

Table 1.3 shows a revised problem space for Cubism, indicating the paired constraints and goal criterion that produced the operators in Table 1.2. Limiting the paired constraints to three again oversimplifies the process, in which constraints proliferate, "generated" as Reitman (1965) said, "from one transformation of the problem to the next" (p. 169).

For example, the promotion of multiple viewpoints tended to produce overly complex cartoons for coloring. This produced the second pair of

---

TABLE 1.2. Problem Space for Cubism Problem

Initial State
  Representational painting styles in 1906.

Operators
  1. If representing an object, fracture and depict it from several viewpoints.
  2. If adding color, limit the number of hues and the range of values.
  3. If representing the relationships between fractured objects, compose a pattern of their parts.

Goal State
  Novel representational painting style, Cubism

TABLE 1.3. Paired Constraints for Cubism Problem

Initial State
  Goal constraint for representational painting in 1906: Paint what you see.

Constraint Pairs
  Preclude   Promote
  1. Single point of view   →   Multiple points of view
  2. Local color   →   Monochromatic palette
  3. Illusion of depth   →   Flat, patterned picture plane

Goal State
  Goal constraint for Cubism in 1914: Paint what you know.

constraints which, by precluding local color (that is, the colors of the objects depicted) and promoting a palette of earth tones, solved the new simplification problem. The third constraint pair which produced rhythmically painted patterns led, in turn, to the inclusion of real patterned materials (newsprint, wallpaper) and the invention of collage.

As the cascade of constraints—all paired and strategically selected—continued, the novel goal criterion (paint what you know) was gradually specified.[1]

The constraints in Table 1.3 structure, in part, the solution path for Braque and Picasso's creativity problem. In cases of influential creativity such as this, a cascading constraint path will—over time—produce a product (painting, sonata, building, novel) that simultaneously defines and meets the new criterion.

In chapter 2, we consider the kinds of constraints involved in the cascade. One of them includes "first choruses."

[1]Notice that selection supposes that the decision-making process, the recognition and retention of generative constraints, is deliberate. It does not preclude the possibility that some things selected are discovered by accident or chance (Austin, 2003). See Appendix A: Learning to Take Chances.

CHAPTER 2

Constraints and First Choruses

What can we learn from Larry Rivers? What else can we learn from Picasso? What else can we learn from Braque?

CONSTRAINTS FOR CONFORMITY

Before describing the kinds of constraints involved in structuring a creativity problem, I want to point out the kind that does hinder novelty. Operators in well-structured problems with single correct solutions, like directions to memorize, calculate exactly, or copy correctly, do the opposite of constraints for creativity. They preclude the surprising and promote the expected, and should be called "constraints for conformity."

CONSTRAINTS FOR CREATIVITY

I like to think of constraints for creativity as *barriers that lead to breakthroughs*. One constraint *precludes* (or limits search among) low-variability, tried-and-true responses. It acts as a barrier which allows the other constraint to *promote* (or direct search among) high-variability, novel responses that could prove to be breakthroughs. The specific pairs are strategically chosen to realize a novel goal criterion (Stokes, 1999a, 2001a, 2001b; Stokes & Fisher, 2005; Stokes & Harrison, 2003).

In the case of Cubism, precluding a privileged viewpoint (the barrier) precipitated the multiplication of viewpoints within a single pictorial space (the breakthrough), allowing the artists to paint more things about their subjects (what they knew) than a single vantage point (what they saw) permitted.

Figure 2.1 shows the four kinds of constraints that we're interested in.

Domain Constraints: First Choruses

Learning and skill acquisition take place within domains, specialized areas of knowledge with agreed-upon performance criteria (Abuhamdeh & Csikzentmihalyi, 2004). The criteria are based on *goal, subject* and *task constraints;* goal constraints specify styles, like Impressionist painting or Baroque music. Subject constraints involve content, landscape and still life in paiting, or major and minor theme in music. Task constraints are concerned with materials and their use—for example, how paint is applied to the canvas, or how ornaments are added to individual notes.

Mastery means substituting knowledge for ignorance, skill for ineptness. When formally trained, novices master constraints in an order determined by others, teachers, coaches, critics. With mastery, a domain becomes what Larry Rivers (1987), a painter and musician, called the *first chorus.* For a representational painter like himself, the "first chorus"—what he improvises on, makes variations of—is the history of painting. In the art museums of any European capital you can watch students copying the masters, practicing their first choruses. In the Museu Picasso in Barcelona, you can see the progress of young Pablo doing the same. If you know what you're looking for, you can see the chromatic character of Titian as well as the palette of Bonnard in the paintings of Mark Rothko.

The transition from master to creator comes when experts impose novel constraints on their domains. As indicated in the Braque-Picasso ex-

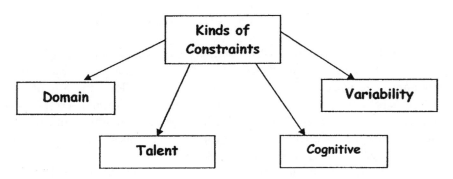

FIGURE 2.1. Kinds of constraints.

ample, the most radical change accompanies a new goal constraint. Substituting what they knew (multiple views/aspects of objects) for what they saw (a single point of view) produced fractured objects *and* a cascade of subsequent subject and task constraints. The prototypical early Cubist subject was a still life. Its contents (subject constraint) were a compote, grapes, pears, wine glasses, sometimes a guitar and sheet music. Task constraints limited colors to neutrals—black, white, browns—which, crossing over the multiplying facets, created surface patterns and restricted depth.

Interestingly, the simplifications following the fracturing reflect two other kinds of constraints—*cognitive* and *variability constraints*. Cognitive constraints, like domain constraints, limit the number of ways something can be done. Variability constraints stipulate how differently it should or must be done.

Cognitive Constraints

This kind of constraint reflects physiological limitations on how many things our brains can process at one time. According to standard memory models, the number of items that can be active in "working memory" at one time is seven plus or minus two. The way to get around that limit is to group or chunk items into larger units. Experts can do extremely complex thinking in their areas of specialization because their knowledge is organized into very large units. Braque and Picasso were already experts in painting when they began to work together on the creativity problem the solution of which was Cubism. This meant they could entertain many painterly ideas at one time, as well as execute many things automatically.

"Automatic" refers to skilled actions. For example, you don't have to think about how to sign your name. Picasso and Braque had the advantage of a huge "first chorus." Neither one had to think about how to draw, compose, or apply color. Braque had the additional advantage of possessing a related repertoire, an expanded first chorus. Having been a house painter, he was skilled in using wallpaper and wood combs. Wallpaper became *papier collés*, printed papers and/or newspapers pasted onto a painting and then drawn or painted over. Wood combs, dipped in one color paint and pulled through another, added the effect of wood grain to the surface.

During what is called the analytic stage of Cubism, when (despite limited contents, colors, and value ranges) the number of viewpoints became impossible to process and the objects depicted became indecipherable, the artists introduced the larger, simpler shapes that become the synthetic variant. Could this too have been due to *cognitive constraints?* Did Braque and

Picasso push the process to the point where even they couldn't work on it without simplification?

It's possible. There's another, based on the third kind of constraint, a *variability constraint.*

Variability Constraints

This kind of constraint specifies how differently something must or should be done. High-variability constraints preclude high-probability, repetitious responses and promote less frequent, even novel, ones in children and adults. Just praise a child for every instance of novelty in painting (a new shape or color mixture) or block–building (a new form) and watch novelty go up (Holman, Goetz, & Baer, 1977). At Barnard, we've even shown that when you acquire a new skill (say painting), you learn *how* to paint, and also *how differently* to continue doing it (Stokes, 1999b). How differently you learn to do something depends on *how difficult* it is to master the skill at hand. Very easy problems don't require trying many things to solve them. More difficult problems do. If early success in doing addition or swinging a bat depends on doing many things, a child will learn to be highly variable when doing math or playing baseball. High variability is important for two reasons. Children who are highly variable learn new things faster than those who are less variable. Adults who are highly variable are more likely to do new things and, as we shall soon see, to keep doing them.

The "how differently" we call *habitual* or *learned variability levels.* Evidence that the levels are learned is two-fold. First, they differ between individuals: Sam shifts among six strategies to solve addition problems; Sally repeatedly uses the same one. Second, they differ between domains for the same individual: Sally is far more variable in painting than in math.

It's easy to come up with your own evidence for learned variability levels. Imagine a situation where the variability requirements are *subjectively* too high. What do you feel?—the discomfort we label anxiety. Now imagine one where the requirements are *subjectively* too low. What do you experience?—the discomfort we call boredom. Importantly, anxiety and boredom motivate us to regain our habitual levels. Said another way, the flip side of a high-variability level is a low boredom threshold (Stokes, 1995).

To avoid boredom, potential creators maintain their habitually high levels of variability by doing many different things in their areas of expertise. In the case of Braque and Picasso, some of those things changed their domain. Both painters had experimented with radically different styles before working together. Braque was an accomplished Fauve, brushing brilliantly high-keyed landscapes in the south of France before teaming up with Picasso in Paris. Picasso was already known for the elongated, emotional, mannerist style portraits of his Blue period. Cubism went through several stages in their joint hands. Once separated, their work changed, but retained Cubist constraints. With Braque, this is more obvious: Shifts in scale and subject matter overpower shifts in style. However, while Picasso initially turned to heroically huge, neoclassical nudes, and produced sculpture, pottery, and prints as well as paintings, the bulk of his subsequent work was based on schematic, patterned, flattened, i.e., Cubist forms. This is not surprising; a great deal of their painting knowledge had become organized around, interconnected with, Cubism.

Talent Constraints

This kind of constraint is in a class of its own. Talents (or gifts) are genetic—you either have them or you don't. You can have them in different degrees; for example, you might be more talented in music and less talented (but still talented) in math. Like all constraints for creativity, talents are two-sided. They simultaneously *promote* and *preclude* interest and skill acquisition in different domains. How interested you are and how easily you acquire a specific skill depends on the brain you're born with.

Extremes are easiest to understand, so let's start with them. Think about the last birthday party you attended. How did the "Happy Birthday" chorus sound? Sort of in-time? Not entirely in-tune? If your answer is yes, your family and friends (like mine, like most) are sort of tone-deaf. They remember (recognize and recall and repeat) the words and the rhythm (the in-time part), but not the pitches (the in-tune part). The opposite of tone-deafness is perfect pitch, the ability to recognize, remember, and replicate exact tones. People with perfect pitch notice sounds, remember sounds, play around with sounds in their head. They're interested in making sounds, in playing instruments. When they take music lessons, they progress faster than other students. Why? For the same reason they were interested in the first place—a "pre-tuned" brain (Winner, 1996).

The same holds for color perception. If you're color blind, pigments—in nature, in art—can't grab your attention or hold your interest. No one studies "perfect hue" (recognizing and remembering and replicating color exactly), but it's something that colorists like Monet or Bonnard seem to have had from the start.

What About the Less-Gifted?

The not-so-good news is that it can take more time and more effort to master the task constraints in their domains. The good news is that, once mastery is achieved, it's difficult to tell an expert who was more gifted from the one who was less gifted (Ericcson, 1996; Sloboda, 1996).

The other good news is that variability levels are learned (Stokes, 2001a). You may be less musical (say, with relative rather than perfect pitch) or have less dexterity than a conservatory classmate. But if you're habitually more variable when composing or performing, you might have a better chance at solving a musical creativity problem.

Does Talent Guarantee Creativity?

No, and for two reasons. The first is tied to those learned variability levels. A high talent level and a low variability level can produce very skillful, very redundant products.

The second reason is that a talent may not be developed. This could happen if it's unrecognized or undervalued (in a family, a community, a culture). In some cases, it might be actively discouraged. Many talents fit in the category economists call "surplus." Too many people have them; too few other people need their products. Sadly, development is sometimes stymied because a talented individual places too much value on novelty. I once heard a student say, "I never read anyone else's verse. I have to find my own voice first." That's certainly a constraint, but eliminating a huge first chorus on which to improvise is *not* a constraint for creativity.

Some people have gifts or talents and not know it because they never had the tools to develop them. Matisse didn't know he had a talent for painting until he was in his twenties, recovering from an illness, and given a paintbox to occupy his time. (We'll talk more about late-bloomers like Matisse in chapters 9 and 10.)

DIFFERENT DOMAINS: DIFFERENT FIRST CHORUSES AND CONSTRAINTS

Each chapter after this one focuses on first choruses and constraints in a different domain. We'll see how several recognized creators precluded their domain's dominant (most rewarded, most recognized) solution (a first chorus) to promote a new one, how some then constrained their own novel solutions, how one pair of constraints leads to another, how the same constraints in different hands lead to different things. We'll also listen to and learn from conversations with less well-known creators whose works are still in progress.

CHAPTER 3

Constraints for Creativity in Literature

What can we learn from Proust? What can we learn from Calvino? What can we learn from Kundera? What can we learn from Byatt? What can we learn from Dillard? What can we learn from Styron? What can we learn from Woolf?

What constraints, including first choruses, help structure the creativity problem in literature?

Novelists, essayists, journalists, writers of prose or poetry are subject to a shared, general set of *task constraints*: audience, organization, grammatical conventions. The idiosyncratic ways in which these are met and modified generate what is called the individual's "voice." Three recognized and recognizable voices—those of Marcel Proust, Milan Kundera, and Italo Calvino—considered, each in his singular way, the same motif, memory. We will see how this *subject constraint* generated a remarkably varied trio of self-imposed specialized *task constraints* that are clearly structural. To do this, Proust, Kundera, and Calvino *precluded* the novel's traditional structure in order to *promote* a trio of novel scaffolds.

The traditional structure is linear, a coherent story line moves forward in time logically progressing from introduction to climax to denouement. For example, for the first sentence, which announces its theme ("Happy families are all alike; every unhappy family is unhappy in its own way,"

Tolstoi (2003, p. 5), *Anna Karenina*—book and title character—presses inexorably toward its climax in chapter XXXI when Anna "thought of the man crushed by the train the day she had first met Vronsky, and she knew what she had to do. With a rapid, light step she went down the steps that led from the tank to the rails and stopped quite near the approaching train (p. 706). Tolstoi brings closure to the novel with Levin's monologue, a quasi-sermon suggesting that survival—of the individual and the family—depends not on happiness, but on goodness.

Precluding the linear promoted novel scaffoldings based on *first choruses* outside the novel and outside the entire domain. We start with the first chorus shared by Proust, Kundera, and Calvino.

The Common First Chorus: Memory

Memory is the product of learning. What does learning produce? Associations, between things in the world, between neurons in the brain. A picture can help. Figure 3.1 represents represents a real apple in the world and its associative network in the brain (McClelland, 2000; McClelland & Rummelhart, 1986).

The visual aspects of our apple are represented by feature detectors, which fire when we see something that's red, round, smooth, and shiny. The same red-round-smooth-shiny pattern lights up in our brains every time we view a real apple or a picture of an apple, and every time we think about

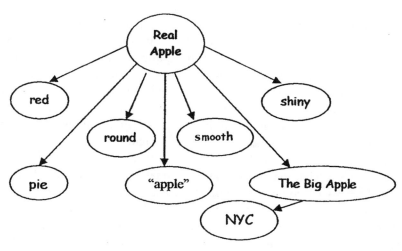

FIGURE 3.1. Apple network.

what an apple looks like. Other things that we learn to associate with apples—such as the word "apple," apple pie or cobbler, caramel or candied apples, Eve and the expulsion from Eden, the Big Apple or New York City expand the network.

Memory is recognizing or calling up (imagining) the apple pattern. This kind of memory is called *semantic*. It stores factual information about the world, which means its accuracy can be checked against the world.

The other kinds of memories, which are also acquired via associations, can't be checked so easily. *Procedural* memory involves the physical—skills like playing an instrument, riding a bike or a skateboard; habits like writing your name, tying your shoelaces—in short, procedures that run off automatically. When you sign your name, do you have to think about how to do it? Do you actually know how you do it?

Emotional memory involves feeling, arousal—what psychologists call "affect." (If you were Snow White, there would be a *big* emotional link in your apple network.)

There are two important things to remember about emotional memory. One is that your current mood affects what you remember (from the past) and what you notice (in the present). Happy moods make enjoyed events more accessible in your memory or more salient and noticeable in the world than sad ones, and vice versa. The other is that things with the same set of features have the same affect. We've all instantly liked or disliked someone. This happens when someone new reminds us—by activating a familiar set of features—of someone else whom we have or had strong feelings about; along with the shared features come the same feelings.

The final kind of memory is *episodic,* memory for personal events. This is (alas!) the least checkable memory of all, and for several reasons. First, like objects, events share features and thus patterns of activation. Repeated events become, as Roger Shank (1990) calls them, "scripts" or models into which different people or places can be slotted. What comes to mind when you think "wedding"? A bride, a groom, a white dress, a bouquet, a march (dum, da, da, da . . . yes, Mendelssohn). You can fill in the rest. After being at or being in many weddings, they merge in memory.

Another reason for the fickleness of personal memories is that every time we retell or elaborate a story about ourselves, the new story becomes part of the associative network, and there is no way to separate the latest version from the original. Even worse, many of our memories are actually other people's stories. What silly stuff did you do at your first birthday party? Mom or Dad can tell you. You can look at photos in the family album. What do *you* remember?

What does this all mean? That memory is both very dependable (we do recognize most things in the world correctly) and very unreliable (we don't get our own pasts right, or even the same way every time). It also explains why it's so hard to understand or "see" anything that's truly new—we don't have the associative networks necessary to recognize, much less to evaluate, the novelty.

TELL ME A STORY: FICTIONS

Providing evidence for the argument that constraints help solve the creativity problem, each of our authors used a different set of *task constraints* to probe and provide scaffolding for different aspects of memory, the shared *subject constraint*. In the following pages we'll explore how Proust's elaborate and endlessly detailed observations are both content and cause of what he called involuntary memory; how Calvino's fracturing of a single experience demonstrates how memory modulates perception, nostalgia, imagination, desire; and how Kundera's musically derived organization details the mechanisms of memory and forgetting.

Proust: Involuntary Memory and the Structure of Myth

À *la recherche du temps perdu* is usually translated as *The Remembrance of Things Past*. An alternative, and more literal translation, which I find closer to my reading of the novel, is *The Search for Lost Time*. The *subject constraint* is memory, but memory of a new kind that the narrator, Marcel, names "involuntary." Thinking about this in problem-solving terms is interesting. Since the kind of memory is new, realizing it, expressing it in writing, represents a new *goal constraint*. To capture (via novel task constraints), and know that he had captured it (the new goal criterion) meant working in (at least initially) an ill-structured problem space.

Proust's involuntary memory cannot be conjured up at will, but is activated when an immediate sensory experience is so closely identifiable (but not identical with—this is not *déjà vu*) with a past one that the past is *re-experienced* (not, as with voluntary memory simply recalled). The famous incident of the petites madeleines is the first of the narrator's re-experiences. Tasting the tea-soaked cake,

> "A shudder ran through me and I stopped, intent upon the extraordinary thing that was happening to me. An exquisite pleasure had invaded my senses, something isolated, detached, with no suggestion of its origin" (Vol. I, p. 48).

The source of the pleasure, he discovers, lies not in the cup at hand, but rather in *sensory memory,* the taste and smell, of Aunt Leonie's equally tea-infused madeleines tasted in his youth, at Combray, on Sunday mornings.

Involuntary memory of this kind precludes simplification, generalization, and promotes elaboration, precision. As *The Search* demonstrates, involuntary memories contain far more specific sensory detail than our apple network.

The other possibility is simpler: many novel things occur. Novelty is important because we only note what surprises us, what is unknown. It takes time, Proust correctly writes, for habit to soften novelty. For example, when the narrator (Marcel) arrives for the first time at Balbec, habit has not yet had time to muffle the percussion of the clock, subdue the violent violet of the drapes, dim the fierce reflections on the glass-fronted bookcases, or soften the stiffness of the starched towel. The sharpness, the harshness, of the not-yet-habitual is obsessed over, elaborated, retained. (Remember that starched towel!)

Proust's attempt to access involuntary memory imposes a novel scaffolding on the *Recherche.* Related, but not identical, events are required. The narrator searches for similarities, for patterns, *and* for specific sensory details that differentiate the repetitions. The scaffolding comes from myth, a literary *first chorus* that predates the novel. The structure of myth is repetitive, reiterative; a story varied in its details is told and retold (Calasso, 1994).

The major Proustian myth involves the tragedy of the human relationship doomed to failure. This relationship, which repeats itself throughout the novel, conjoins two sets of almost interchangeable characters. The first includes M. Swann, the Marquis de St. Loup, the Baron Charlus, and the narrator. Each suffers the same obsessive jealousy over his Odette, Rachel, Albertine, or Morel, all of whose affections are entirely selfish, dependent on the satisfaction of their needs. When the narrator speaks of Swann's "anxious, tormenting need, whose object is the person alone, an absurd, irrational need, which the laws of this world make impossible to satisfy and difficult to assuage—the insensate, agonizing need to possess exclusively" (Proust, 1871/1982, Vol. I, p. 252), he is also speaking of himself, his friend Robert, and his friend's uncle. The relationship is experienced in succession by everyone, at different points in time (the pattern)—and the book—swells with the specifics of each recurrence (the variants).

Habit ultimately provides (successive) respite for the jealous protagonists. Just as Swann ceases loving Odette, and Robert ceases to love Rachel, the narrator knows he will no longer love Albertine once he has become habituated to her absence.

Figure 3.2 diagrams the involuntary, sensory memory that both con-cludes—and Proust tells us at the end, instigated—the book. Notice that there is a towel and a napkin.

You already know about that towel. What of the napkin? Sharing "the same degree of stiffness and starchedness as the towel with which I had found it so awkward to dry my face as I stood in front of the window on the first day of my arrival at Balbec . . .", it evokes a complete sensory, com-pletely involuntary memory, including "the plumage of an ocean green and blue like the tail of a peacock. And . . . not merely those colours, but the whole instant of my life on whose summit they rested . . ." (Proust, 1871/1982, Vol. III, p. 901)

What Can We Learn From Proust?

The way a novel *goal constraint* precludes traditional task constraints and promotes novel ones, includes *first choruses* outside the genre in which a writer works. The scaffolding for a new conception of memory was mythic in origin. Repetition with intensely detailed variation produced the net-works that evoked, made possible, the experience of involuntary memory, the actual recovery, the reliving of *temps perdu*.

Calvino and Kundera: Memory and Modernism

Modernist fiction, like Cubist painting, draws our attention to surfaces, not depths; to patterns, not particulars; to structures, not sentiments. The world becomes a complex diagram, in which characters are types, neither central nor individual, more interesting intellectually than emotionally.

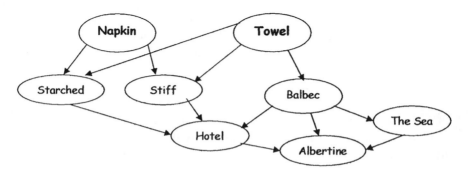

FIGURE 3.2. Proust's network.

Mentioning neither Calvino nor Kundera, Annie Dillard (1982) describes the difficulties that these shared constraints—surface, structure, pattern—present to the reader. Texts which "stress pattern over reference," she writes, "baffle a reader until he locates or composes a provisional dictionary, a set of terms defined internally by the text" (p. 52). What are these but new problem spaces?

Kundera (1988), in fact, tells us that his novels are searches for some evasive definitions. Each is "based on a set of fundamental words which are analyzed, studied, defined, redefined, and thus transformed into categories of existence" (p. 84). Memory, too, is categorical: red, round, smooth, and shiny are attributes/words that comprise the category "apple." Kundera's dictionary is organized musically; Calvino's visually.

Calvino: Visual Memory, Nostalgia, and Desire

Calvino (1993) explicitly concurred with the premise of this book. He wrote that "the construction of a novel according to strict rules, to *constraints* [italics added], by no means limits freedom as a storyteller, but stimulate it" (p. 123).

Calvino's *task constraints* arose from his fondness for *first choruses* outside literature—geometric form, symmetry, numbered series, combinations. The form that symbolizes combination best is the crystal.

> For me the main thing in a narrative is not the explanation of an extraordinary event, but the *order of things* that this extraordinary event produces in itself and around itself; the pattern, the symmetry, the network of images deposited around it, as in the formation of a crystal (Calvino, 1986, p. 73).

Order and pattern scaffold Calvino's stories. The extraordinary event in *Invisible Cities* is the extended visit of Marco Polo to China. Polo arrived in 1275 at the court of the Khan and stayed 16 years. During three of these years, he was the governor of the city of Yangzhou; during another three—the three on which Calvino focuses—he was in the Khan's diplomatic service, an agent sent to different parts of the empire.

The Khan and Polo have 18 conversations, all in the gardens of the palace, all ostensibly about the cities of the empire that Polo visits in order to describe them. Why this mission? Historically, because the empire is endless and formless: The Khan can only discern its pattern through his envoy's accounts, and fictionally, because the network of images arises from the brief, but fantastically detailed descriptions of 55 imperial cities.

The network, like all memories, is an associative one. Indeed, the Khan notices that "Marco Polo's cities resembled one another, as if the passage from one to another involved not a journey, but a change of elements" (p. 44), and Polo observes that in "traveling, you realize that all differences are lost: each city takes to resembling all cities, places exchange their form, order, distances . . ." (p. 137). Possible cities are combinations of these elements.

The pattern of the city, if not the empire, can be traced in the similarities of the 55 cities to each other and, more critically, to the one city never overtly described, but at the basis of each description, Venice. Venice is the crystal that is fractured and multiplied, because Polo can only notice, and the Khan can only imagine, things that are already known, already in the associative networks named memory.

What is the network around Venice? This is the 13th century. Venice is a Byzantine city, its architectural center the multiple arches and domes, the glittering mosaic and marbled surfaces, and the incense-shadowed recesses of St. Mark's. Venice is a maritime city, ringed by canals and bridges; a trading city, divided into specialized quarters; a city of pleasure, courtesans, and carnivals. The images are the dictionary that defines the know-able world.

Look at the network. It shows what Polo finally tells the Khan, "Every time I describe a city, I am saying something about Venice" (p. 86). Among the cities he describes are Diomira, with its 60 silver domes that resemble the golden ones of St. Mark's, and Dorethea, with its drawbridges and canals and quarters specializing in "goods that each family hold in monopoly—bergamot, sturgeon roes, astrolabes, amethysts" (p. 9). Anastasia too is watery, a city of concentric canals, rich in the trading of chalcedony, agate, and chrysoprase. In Phyliss, Polo tells the Khan, "You rejoice in observing all the bridges over the canals, each different from the others: cambered, covered, on pillars, on barges, suspended, with tracery balustrades" (p. 90).

The network (Figure 3.3) includes, from the Khan's atlas, one of the still-to-be-built cities, existing only in plan. These plans, too, resemble Venice: "the city in the shape of Amsterdam, a semicircle facing north, with concentric canals" and "the city in the shape of New Amsterdam . . . with streets like deep canals" (p. 139).

What Can We Learn From Calvino?

Two important things. First, that different *goal constraints* demand different task constraints. Proust's narrator saw the same relationship in every relationship; Calvino's, the same city in every city. The differences are somewhat paradoxical. Marcel's repetitions (Odette-Swann, Rachel-St.Loup,

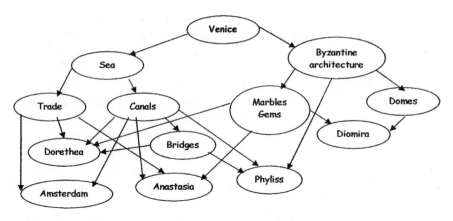

FIGURE 3.3. Calvino's network.

Albertine-Marcel; the napkin and towel) are emotional but orderly, following each other as they would in real time. Polo's are intellectual but unordered, following no logical sequence, providing instead "a network in which one can follow multiple routes and draw multiple, ramified conclusions" (Calvino, 1993, p. 71).

Second, that expertise from outside domains can provide critical *first choruses* to influence and expand the one in which you work.

Kundera: Music and the Mechanisms of Memory

Marcel and Marco Polo remember because they repeat and elaborate. Repetition and elaboration strengthen the connections between things remembered. In *Slowness,* Kundera (1996) constructs a dictionary, not of things remembered, but of *mechanisms* for remembering and forgetting.

Kundera's dictionary–definition of the novel—a search for some fugitive, evasive definitions—is itself a new *goal constraint.* The words in search of meaning he quite purposefully calls themes. The meaning of "theme" here is simultaneously literary and musical; Kundera's inquiry about a topic takes the form of a musical composition. *Slowness* interweaves two themes, defined by tales of dual seductions that take place at the same chateau, but in different centuries. The style in which one tale is told typifies the titular theme, slowness; the style of the other, its opposite, speed.

The primary *task constraint* here is polyphonic—the two independent, equally important themes are presented at the same time. This simultaneity is required because the meaning of each theme (slowness and speed) depends on its interaction and contrast with the other theme. The major contrast in *slowness* is presented as a set of equations: "The degree of slowness is directly proportional to the intensity of memory; the degree of speed is directly proportional to the speed of forgetting" (Kundera, 1996, p. 39). This will give us the first two nodes in our memory model—slowness and speed, with their respective links to remembering and forgetting (see Figure 3.4).

The two major themes are represented by fewer or more characters, in fewer or more chapters, with fewer or more incidents, and in sentences of fewer or more words. The number of words not only establishes different tempi, it is also directly related to memory. (Remember that capacity limit?) Another equation, this one from psychology: the more things experienced, the more likely the system will be overloaded, and the fewer things will be remembered.

There are only two actors to illuminate the slowness category. These are characters in a supposed 18th century novel, Madame de T. and the Young Chevalier. An elaborate, multi-phrase sentence structure slows the tempo both of their interaction and our attention.

We never hear Madame de T. speak, but we hear that her speech is artful . . . "the fruit of an art, the art of conversation, which lets no gesture pass without comment and works over its meaning" (p. 32). Hers is the voice of Epicurus, preaching—and practicing—hedonism, the philosophy of avoiding pain by moderating pleasure. This takes both planning and discretion. Madame de T. devises an architectonic structure to the sole night that she spends with the Chevalier,

> a night shaped like a triptych, a night as an excursion in three stages: first, they walk in the park; next, they make love in a pavilion; last, they continue the lovemaking in a secret chamber of the chateau. At daybreak they separate (p. 5).

Why this imposition of form on time? Both beauty and memory demand it, the narrator explains. "Conceiving their encounter as a form was especially precious for them, since their night was to have no tomorrow and could be repeated only through recollection" (p. 15).

Moderation, elaboration, structure, slowness, memory: an elegant, easy-to-recall category. The one for speed is too cluttered. There are too many "dancers," as the one 20th century Epicurean, Pontevin, calls them, seeking to take over the stage. They are gathered at Madame de T.'s chateau, now turned into a convention center. Since they are too many, they create too many, too short incidents, with too many interruptions. No one has a

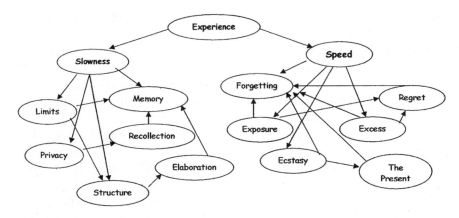

FIGURE 3.4. Kundera's network.

complete night to share. A diagram of this would quickly become daunting. To simplify, we will consider a single coupling.

In contrast to the Madame-Chevalier liaison, which is uninterrupted, private, sensual, memorable, Vincent and Julie's night is splintered, public, obscene, an embarrassment to be forgotten—and quickly. Since there is no privacy, a liaison is actually not possible; in public, on stage, a dancer's words and actions are directed at the audience, not the partner. But why the relation between publicity and obscenity? Again, the narrator explains:

> A word uttered in a small enclosed space has a different meaning from the same word resonating in an amphitheater. No longer is it a word for which he holds full responsibility and which is addressed exclusively to the partner, it is a word that other people demand to hear, people who are there, looking at them. True, the amphitheater is empty, but even though it is empty, the audience, imagined and imaginary, potential and virtual, is there, is with them (p. 16).

The Epicurean who avoids suffering by moderating pleasure enjoys the pleasure of nostalgia; the dancer—drawn to excess and exposure—escapes regret by forgetting. At the end of their respective nights, the Chevalier and Vincent both leave the Chateau. The first is carried off slowly in his chaise, with time enough and privacy enough to recollect his night. The second speeds off on his motorcycle, focusing solely on his moment of flight, alone, yes, but "cut off from both the past and the future . . . wrenched from the continuity of time" (p. 2), and from memory, which requires time for recollection, repetition, elaboration.

What Can We Learn From Kundera?

Something that we've seen both in Braque and Calvino, the importance of *first choruses* outside your working domain. The primary constraint for Kundera is his novel-as-dictionary idea. *Sans* Kundera's musical "first chorus," definition as a *goal constraint* might have created variations on literary structures: definitions in alphabetical order (a traditional dictionary), definition by relationship or replacement (a traditional thesaurus). With music in his repertoire, Kundera created *task constraints*—riffs and rhythmic scaffoldings from which—in time, in specific times—his elusive definitions emerge.

TELL ME YOUR STORY: MEMOIR

Domain-changing constraints, like Proust's, Calvino's or Kundera's "novel" scaffolds, are rare. Less rare are constraints that generate novelty in highly malleable forms like memoir writing.

Memoir has three basic constraints. The *subject constraint* precludes autobiography; a memoir is not a whole life. It's more like an album, a prose album, in which the writer places snapshots-in-words from his or her life. The snapshots are selected, edited, arranged by theme, by time, past or present. Memoir, like memory, is selective, its seductiveness dependent on the details selected.

There are two *task constraints*. One involves *sincerity* or degree of truthfulness. Memoirs involve episodic memories, which are notoriously unreliable. What *really* happened? To what extent is the writer reconstructing, reconstruing the facts? A. S. Byatt's (1993) answer is "a lot." Writing, she says, "does not eat up life, reality, truth, it rearranges it so that it is forever unrecognizable except in terms of the fixed form, the set arrangement" (p. 18).

Snapshots are descriptions; sincerity aims at, approximates, accuracy. Both lead to a second task constraint, on how *materials* (words) are used. One way involves *mimesis,* which aims directly at truths about things, using words that describe or denote them. Mimesis may be used almost exclusively (as in Virginia Woolf, Annie Dillard, or William Styron) or it can be mixed with metaphor (as in Byatt), which shows us indirect truths, relationships between a thing and another thing.

Snapshots of Time: Woolf and Dillard

The same task constraint, mimesis, produced vastly different effects in Woolf and Dillard. Woolf's descriptions are elegant and elaborate, painterly and plush with adjectives strung together by semi-colons. In Dillard, they seem simpler; there are semi-colons, but the voice is more active, immediate, American.

A *Sketch of the Past,* Woolf (1940/1970) tells us, begins with the first memory. She actually reports two memories, both consisting not of words, but of sensations—things seen, things heard, things felt. These are, in fact, the earliest possible memories.

The things seen included flowers. Some were reproductions, like the ones on her mother's dress, "red and purple flowers on a black ground . . . I was on her lap. I therefore saw the flowers she was wearing very close; and can still see purple and red and blue, I think, against the black; they must have been anemones" (p. 64). Others were real, like the ones outside her nursery, "passion flowers growing on the wall . . . great starry blossoms, with purple streaks, and large green buds, half empty, half full" (p. 66).

The things heard included

> "waves breaking, one, two, one, two, and sending a splash of water on the beach; and then breaking, one, two, one, two, behind a yellow blind . . . [and] the blind draw its little acorn across the floor as the wind blew the blind out" (pp. 64–65).

Woolf goes on to characterize early memory exactly: "I am hardly aware of myself, but only of the sensation. I am only the container of the feeling. . . . Perhaps this is characteristic of all childhood memories; perhaps it accounts for their strength" (p. 67).

What Can We Learn From Woolf?

That the earliest memories are Proustian: sensory, primarily visual; when auditory, without words. If your *goal constraint* is to capture an early memory, Woolf's way with mimesis, her painterly prose—embellished, ornamented, baroque in its extravagance of detail—provides a rich model.

Annie Dillard recalled somewhat later memories, allowing her both to notice things and to note the categories or classes to which they belonged. For Dillard, a class can be as simple, and as large, as "things that are active and exciting." *An American Childhood* (1990) begins when Dillard was five.

Life was immediate and eventful, parsed by the author into piled-up phrases that mimic the movement. In the mornings,

> . . . men left in a rush: they flung on coats, they slid kisses at everybody's cheeks, they slammed car doors; they ground their car starters till the motors caught with a jump. And the Catholic schoolchildren left in a rush; I saw them from our dining-room windows. They burst into the street buttoning their jackets; they threw dry catalpa pods at the stop sign and at each other. They hugged their brown-and-tan workbooks to them, clumped and parted, and proceeded toward St. Bede's school almost by accident (pp. 285–286).

Mimesis is equally agile at probing unknowns, like the bogeyman-in-the-bedroom;

> When I was five . . . I would not go to bed willingly because something came into my room. This was a private matter between me and it. If I spoke of it, it would kill me. . . . It was a transparent, luminous oblong (p. 291).

or the rites of school passage.

> Whatever we needed in order to meet the future, it was located at the un-thinkable juncture of Latin class and dancing school (p. 365).

What Can We Learn From Dillard?

That later memories can be caught in wider nets, grouped into categories. How Dillard's kind of mimesis captures her categorizing. Dillard (1982) refers to her style as plain prose. Plain prose easily presents and replicates rhythms.

Re-read the short quote about the early morning rush. Read it aloud. Notice how it rushes right along. Notice too how sparse and precise the sentences are. It is very difficult to write well in plain prose. There is no place to hide.

Snapshots With Themes: Byatt and Styron

Snapshots in time can spread wide nets. Snapshots with themes are both more compact and more elaborated, interconnected, patterned. The primary *task constraint* here is patterning. Parental deaths—Byatt's father, Styron's mother—fuse the immediate with the shared ways of speaking or acting that permeate and sustain family itself.

Byatt's scaffolding is metaphoric. The title identifies the metaphor, *Sugar* (1992). In the first sentence, Byatt tells us that her mother "had a respect for truth, but she was not a truthful woman. . . . She lied in small matters, to tidy up embarrassments, and in larger matters, to avoid unpalatable truths" (p. 215). Metaphor enlarges on mimesis: her mother's accounts were "like pearls, or sugar-coated pills, grit and bitterness polished into roundness by comedy" (p. 229).

Sugar permeates, providing a path through, a pattern for, the story. It is the father's family's business. Byatt herself admits to selecting and confecting: "What is all this, all this story so far but a careful selection of things that can be told, things that can be arranged in the light of day?"(p. 241). Even her father, a judge, with a judge's great respect for evidence, truth, and justice, constructed "a tale, a myth, a satisfactory narrative of his life" (p. 251). But tales are necessities, because the actual moment is inaccessible, at least to words. Only "after things have happened, when we have taken a breath and a look, we begin to know what they are and were, we begin to tell them to ourselves" (p. 248).

What Can We Learn From Byatt?

How metaphor—a *task constraint*—can connect, clarify, and create memories. Create, not re-create, because the networks crafted by the metaphor, the common theme, are new and their connections newly experienced.

Styron shows us a different kind of connecting and supporting structure. His scaffoldings partition present and past, each with a distinct voice. This *task constraint* collapses his family history (escaping from each other) into a single day, *A Tidewater Morning* (1993).

The morning is reported in the boy's voice, in regular type:

> I recall that walk with the shine of reality . . . I recall the morning's headlines with the same clarity that I recall any of the major wars, assassinations, bombings . . . that were spread across the front pages as the century plunged onward . . . PRAGUE AWAITS HITLER ULTIMATUM (p. 126).

The history is revealed by the parental voices, in italics, in snippets of past arguments, prior escapes from each other's differences. One reveals the mother's regrets,

> *If I had married Charlie Winslow . . . I'm sure that he would have taken me to Paris . . . I might have even had one Chanel gown, as well as the father's stoicism, Then I'm sorry you settled for so little, Adelaide. I never promised you riches. . . . I've always admired much in you. But I can't admire your inability to understand that my own passions are not of tangible objects, but, if you'll pardon my saying so, of the spirit and the intellect (p. 100).*

As the pattern alternates (between the long-concluded conversations and the day's description), disjoints in the relationships reveal themselves. Father, mother, and son each experience the world in his or her own way. At the end, father and son escape, *each in his own way* (the repeated difference in the relatings), from the mother's death. The father repeats the biblical phrase that comforts *him*. The son distracts himself from father and mother with "other words. . . . "My name is Paul Whitehurst, it is the eleventh of September, 1938, when Prague Awaits Hilter Ultimatum" (p. 142).

What Can We Learn From Styron?

That patterns are powerful because they can reveal the associative maps that make up memories. Stryon's parsing of present and past in different voices is the scaffold that creates and sustains his pattern. Like Proust's, the pattern is recognizable because it is repetitive. Unlike Proust's, it is repeated by the same, rather than different, people. Repetition takes many literary forms.

A CONVERSATION:
CONSTRAINTS CAN BE CRIMINAL

The mystery is a literary genre with a well-established set of *domain constraints* (see Figure 3.5). Paul Grescoe, a writer of detective novels, described some of these, as well as his ways of working *within* and *against* them. All words, phrases, sentences in quotation marks are from Paul's

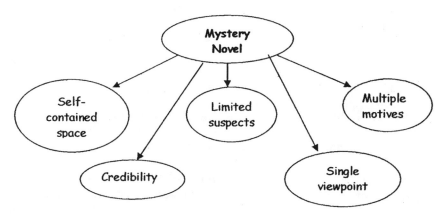

FIGURE 3.5. Criminal constraints.

very long and detailed e-mail response (June 27, 2001) to a request for his contribution to my book. The brackets inside the quotes are my additions.

> "From the first," he wrote, "I've accepted some of the conventions of the mystery, chief among them the concept *[subject constraint]* of having a selected group of characters interact in a contained universe. Classic examples are the country house where Londoners gather for a weekend or the express train rocketing across Europe with a cargo of passengers linked in some yet-to-be-determined way."

Oh yes, I said to myself, "Death on the Nile."

Working *within* the self-contained space constraint, Paul has confined his characters to a movie set in Vancouver (*Flesh Wound,* 1991), a Japanese ship cruising to Alaska (*Blood Vessel, 1993*). Working *against* the constraint in order to "stretch the confines of both realms," he's introduced "outsiders: local hookers and pimps to the visiting members of the movie company; environmentalists and business people to the usual cruise-ship passenger roll."

Another

> typical constraint of the detective novel is the first-person narrator who lets the reader see and know only what he/she observes. It's effective because the lone wolf's viewpoint tends to contain the amount and variety of information the reader is being offered at any one time. It's frustrating because it's difficult to communicate motivations (Grescoe).

One way around the constraint, which Paul calls "old and hoary," is having the detective discover another character's diary. Another, found in "Flesh Wound," is to "create a couple of sidekicks, a Hollywood stuntman and a woman reporter . . . who could go off on their own and return with fresh information" (Grescoe).

In a still-being-written book, (Grescoe, manuscript in preparation) Paul says he wants to

> push the envelope even further and have several third- or possibly first-person chapters describing the actions and thoughts of a villain, chapters that will sandwich between those written in the detective's voice and allow me to present a fuller portrait of the character whose motivations are usually explained only at the climax, when his/her identity is revealed.

A third subject constraint is the single villain. Working *against* this, Grescoe's books have more than a single killer, each with a different motive. "Of course," he wrote, "in *Murder on the Orient Express,* Agatha Christie took this multi-villainy to wonderfully absurd heights."

A final constraint, which all mystery writers must meet, is credibility. Unless the details are right, the "reader's suspension of disbelief would be strained." So when Grescoe was writing *Flesh Wound,* he "talked to transsexuals, read books by and about them, and passed the final manuscript to Canada's leading transgender surgeon for checking." (Interestingly, authenticating the details allows a writer to be inventive in other ways.)

> Held to account by insuring that the physical details were accurate, I let myself go in imagining the psychological pain that went along with the desire to change sex and invented a revealing diary for the man/woman I'd created. In many ways this was the most satisfying part of the novel for me and readers have commented on its creativity.

WHAT HAVE WE LEARNED?

How *first choruses* from different genres (myth for Proust) and from different domains (mathematics for Calvino, music for Kundera) can help change the one in which someone is working.

How, and how far, constraints help structure the creativity problem in literature. How far depends on the *goal constraint* (realizing novel concepts of memory) of the writer. We've seen how *task constraints* expand a domain by creating new kinds of scaffolds (Proust, Calvino, Kundera) to meet those goals. This is the kind of creativity we call "influential."

We've also looked at how novelty can be created using *task constraints* in well-established forms (Woolf, Dillard, Byatt, Styron). This is the kind of creativity we call "generative." It appears in the mystery as well as the memoir, and—as Paul Grescoe's communication with this writer shows—is generated by working *with,* and *against* a genre's current *first choruses.*

CHAPTER 4

Constraints for Creativity in Art

What can we learn from Monet? What can we learn from Matisse? What can we learn from Rothko? What can we learn from Cezanne? What can we learn from Bartlett? What can we learn from Johns? What can we learn from Warhol?

What constraints structure the creativity problem in art? Producing any painting (or work on paper, including print, collage, water color, and the like) involves placing *subject constraints* on content, for example portrait or still-life, and *task constraints* on materials and working methods. For most painters, most constraints are *first choruses:* given by teachers, suggested by the past, taken from the popular. Producing a new kind of painting involves creating a series of novel constraints. To show this, we will look, in some depth, at three creators who began with a similar subject constraint, but, via each one's subsequent series of unique constraints, produced radically different masterworks. Each one's first chorus will be included.

A quicker sketch compares past and contemporary painters who share a constraint introduced by Monet: the multiple, a series that shares content and composition, but differs in execution. One such series by Monet included 24 paintings depicting the same row of poplars at different times of day.

A conversation with a painter closes the chapter. All the illustrations are my much-simplified versions of the originals.

CONSTRAINING SUBJECT: SEEING THE LIGHT

Three painters whose mature oeuvres focused on the effects of light were Claude Monet, Henri Matisse, and Mark Rothko. Monet wanted to render the immediate impression of what he called the "envelope" of things; Matisse, a condensation of that impression; Rothko, the expressive quality of light, the response removed from any particular impression. These disparate *goal constraints* drove their creative endeavors in different directions, but by similar processes.

For each, *goal* (impression, condensation, or expression) and *subject* (light) *constraints* led to *task constraints* on currently accepted material conventions. Each then constrained his own novel solutions, leading to the late, great (in style and in size) works. Matisse was very clear about the necessity of such change. "When you have exploited the possibilities that lie in one direction, you must", he wrote, "change course, search for something new. . . . If I had continued down the old road, which I knew so well, I would have ended up as a mannerist" (Flam, 1995, p. 75).

Before we talk about each painter separately, a few words on light. Light has three properties that painters exploit. The first is *hue,* which is what we usually mean when we say "color." Prisms and rainbows separate light into seven hues: red is the name given to the longest light wave we can see; violet is the name of the shortest. We'll use hue and color interchangeably. The other two aspects are *value* and *saturation.* Value refers to lightness and darkness; saturation to intensity. Pure, unmixed colors are more saturated than combinations.

Monet and Impressionism

In contrast to Cubism's credo, "paint what you know," Impressionism's goal criterion was "paint what you see." This was its novel and primary *goal constraint.* Remember the apple-network from the previous chapter? What you *know* is the pattern of feature detectors in your brain associated with the category "apple." What you *see* are the separate, specialized feature detectors for the individual hues, highlights, contours, and surfaces of this specific apple.

The painter who follows Monet's advice forgets, ignores in effect, the object, focusing instead on patches of color—squares of blue, oblongs of pink, streaks of yellow (Morgan, 1996). If you try this, you'll see that it actually makes representation easier, because you're constructing a painting the way the retina constructs the visual world.

First Choruses

During Monet's apprenticeship, the dominant domain criteria for representational painting involved contrasting values. Lights modulated into darks. Darks were murky browns and blacks. Even Monet painted this way. The waves in the "Mouth of the Seine at Honfleur" (1865)[1] are earth-colored—raw umber, burnt sienna.

The more critical first chorus was scientific. Impressionism started with the scientific study of sensation, in particular the color wheel designed by Chevreul, a French chemist (Forge, 1995; Patin, 1993: Seitz, 1982). Chevreul's wheel presented color as a set of relationships between the four primary hues (the warmer red and yellow, the cooler blue and green) and their intermediaries. Monet's initial, and initially ill-defined, goal was to present the world as a set of color relationships: this is how light breaks up, this is how the fleeting moment looks (Stokes, 2001). To accomplish this, he devised a *series of constraints,* first on his domain's current criteria, and then on his own.

Phase One: Constraining Value

The first *goal constraint* was representing how light breaks up on things. The *task constraints* followed: the first constrained carefully modeled value contrasts. Precluding contrasts between different degrees of light and dark promoted contrasts between different hues. Using colors with more and more closely related values placed a second, derived constraint on another convention, sharply delineated shapes. The result was softer, indistinct edges.

How does light break up on things? In "Regata at Sainte-Addresse" (1867), in bright clear contrasting hues—cream sails casting Prussian blue shadows on a teal–green sea. In front of the "Hotel des Roches Noires, Trouville" (1870), in the quick separate strokes of a color sketch—red, cream, and blue patches become three flags and the sky and clouds behind, beside, between them. The patches came from a constraint that Monet placed on conventional paint application. Instead of first filling in the sky or sand, and then adding clouds or flags, he lay down a mosaic of colors,

---

[1]All dates for Monet's paintings are taken from Wildenstein (1996a, 1996b).

intermingling dabs of cobalt, curls of lead–white, scattered spots of vermilion, so that light flickered across their surface.

Phase Two: Constraining Motif

The second, more elusive *goal constraint* concerned what Monet called the *enveloppe*, the constantly changing atmosphere. The problem became representing how light breaks up between things. To do this, Monet constrained his motif or subject in a way that turned repetition into variation. Precluding change *of* motif promoted change *in* the motif.

In 1891, Monet set his easel down in a field and painted 23 canvases named for the objects (the grainstacks) in them and the envelope (the effects) around them. He sat in a boat near Giverny and painted a second series, 24 paintings again named for similar objects (poplars) and differing effects (in overcast weather, at dusk, evening, sunset, in the spring, in the autumn, in the wind).

How does light break up between things? In "Grainstack at Sunset," (1889) into the same hues—yellow, pink, blue, lavender—everywhere. The envelope is continuous: It may be glaringly bright in sky, field, and hill, and darker, cooler in the shadow of the stack, but it has no local color. Paint application and finish are further constrained. The surface is a dense, uninterrupted web of color. Monet's brushstrokes, still separate, are layered, inter-woven. In "The Four Trees," (1891) color—and with it focus, attention—is again scattered everywhere and at once. There is still a point of view, but it is no longer privileged. Soon even it would be constrained.

Phase Three: Constraining Things

Monet's last series, the "Grand Decorations" (1914–20) are paradoxical: the *goal constraint* neither precluded nor required things. Lilies and pads, wisteria and willows, were only—to use Monet's word—accompaniments (Morgan, 1998). The motif was the invisible mirror, the continuously shifting, reflective surface of the pond. The *goal constraint* was deceptively simplified: representing how light—by itself, not on things or between things—breaks up.

The studies for the decorations amplified earlier constraints on depth, definition, finish, point of view, focus. In the early series paintings, Monet looked at light from a middle distance. Now, he moved up very close (precluding depth), making his close-ups very big (precluding easel-sized canvas), and broadly stroked, with scumbled, thickly layered, not-always-filled-in surfaces (precluding finish).

In "Water Lilies, Reflections of Weeping Willows" (c. 1916), we no longer look from the shore, but from above the pond and very close to its surface. We look at fragments; lily-pads, horizontally, summarily stroked in dark saturated blue-greens, with magenta outlines that fall outside or over the blue-greens; reflections represented by separated vertical strokes, darker greens and blacks for the willows, lighter lavender for the sky. Things are not clearly separated. The lavender is under and on top of everything. It even falls inside the magenta outlines of the lily-pads.

It's instructive to compare compositions from the series and the "Grand Decorations." "Poplars" (1891) (see left panel, Figure 4.1) shows four trees reflected in the Seine. In "Water Lilies," (1919–20) (see right panel, Figure 4.1) we see only the reflecting surface of Monet's pond. The pale lavenders, blues, greens, and yellows are very close in value. Separateness is constrained. The scattered strokes of white might be the lilies or their reflections.

In paintings like "Reflections of Clouds on the Water-Lily Pond" (c. 1920), there are no more "things." Precluding things promoted pure fields of color. By itself at last, Monet's light broke up into atmospheric abstractions too new to be understood by his contemporaries, influential 25 years later when the Abstract and Lyric Expressionists claimed Monet as their first chorus.

There's a lot to say about Monet—and a lot to learn. Since I'm a visual learner, I like to make charts that organize and summarize what I want to remember. Table 4.1 is my Monet chart, divided into goal, subject, and task constraints.

What Can We Learn From Monet?

Not many painters change their domains multiple times, but Monet shows that it *can* be done and, importantly, teaches us *how.*

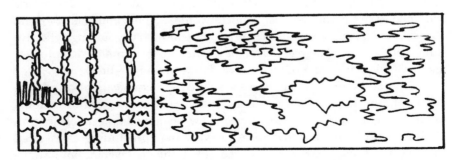

FIGURE 4.1. Contour renderings of "Poplars" (1891) and "Water Lilies" (1919–20).

TABLE 4.1. Monet's Constraints

Goal (Sub-goals)	Subject	Task
Show how light breaks up		
1. *on things*	(none)	Preclude *value contrasts* → promote contrasting *hues*
		Preclude hard *edges* → promote *merging* objects
		Preclude *continuous* paint application → promote *mosaic* of strokes, hue
2. *between things*	Preclude *change* in motif → promote *series* of same motif	Preclude *local color* → promote *same hues everywhere*
		Preclude *mosaic* → promote *scumbled, layered* paint
		Preclude *point of view* → promote *scattering of attention*
3. *by itself*	Preclude *things* → promote *color fields*	Preclude *depth* → promote extreme *close-up*
		Preclude small *easel-size* canvases → promote *mural-size painting*
		Preclude *objects* → promote *continuity*

For Monet, *how* involved two things. The first was creating a *series of constraints,* precluding, first, the domain's criteria, and second, the artist's own successful variations. The first goal constraint in Monet's chart precluded the criteria for representational painting in the 1860s, that is, dark-light contrasts. The second and third goal constraints precluded Monet's own criteria.

How also involved *strategic constraint selection,* specific to a current goal, pairing what was precluded and what was promoted. To realize his second goal constraint, Monet didn't simply superimpose the color of the *enveloppe* on the objects it surrounded. To learn how light breaks up between things, he replaced the colors of each object with the shared colors of the atmosphere. Notice, too, how one task constraint necessitates—leads to—others. Once objects have a common coloration, it acts like camouflage. Focusing on any one thing becomes difficult, is precluded. Monet redirects our attention, in multiple directions.

Something else to be learned from Monet's series is what it doesn't involve. That's change-for-change's sake. Too many young artists today aren't getting (from gatekeepers) or taking (for themselves) the time necessary to develop a new style, a new set of constraints (Kimmelman, 2000). Monet explored how light broke up on things, his first goal constraint, for 20 years. (It took Braque and Picasso eight years, working together, to develop Cubism.)

Finally, there's an important question we haven't asked of Monet. The question involves motivation. Why did Monet keep changing his constraints, why didn't he stick to, get stuck in, any one successful solution. We'll answer that question in chapter 10 when we discuss the relationships between early apprenticeships and variability levels.

Matisse and Fauvism

Different ends require different means. Monet aimed to paint what he saw; Matisse, the impact of what he saw. The credo, the *goal constraint,* changed from "paint what you see" to "paint what you feel about what you see." In the process, Matisse's palette shifted from observed, soft, and closely valued hues to exaggerated, intense, abruptly contrasting ones; from perceived to pure colors; from impression to expression. "A pot of colors flung in the public's face," complained one critic (Elderfield, 1976, p. 43).

First Choruses

Earlier pots of paint—each part of Matisse's first chorus—had been flung. There was Monet, of course, rejecting modulation of dark and light. There was Gaughin, radically rejecting perspective, flattening forms with bold outlines and bolder colors. There was Van Gogh, replacing local color with expressive color.

Unlike Monet, whose goal changed over time (how light breaks up on things, between things, by itself), Matisse's *goal constraint* was constant, stated early and clearly: an art of pure color and pure line (Schneider, 1984). Each phase in his career represents not a shift in goal but a clarification of that goal. In each, the great draftsman devised a new task constraint on conventional, painterly ways of using color.

Phase One: Drawing With Color

The first *task constraint* precluded the preliminary oil sketch, sepia-toned, value-contrasted. Working together at Collioure in 1905,[2] Matisse and Derain began to draw on canvas with pure, saturated hues, leaving blatantly bare spaces of canvas between their bright, scattered, slashed brushmarks (Leymarie, 1955).

Precluding the preparatory sketch promoted a different kind of finished painting. The trees in "Landscape at Collioure" (1905) (see left panel, Figure 4.2) have bright orange curves for trunks, and separate, intense green, blue, and yellow strokes for boughs. Another landscape shows Madame Matisse, her robe a swirl of blue and purple lines, a green shadow on her face, reading beside a stream of disjunct red, green, yellow, and purple lozenges.

Pierre Schneider (1984) aptly called this phase of Fauvism "destruction by color" (p. 215). What was destroyed was the realistic representation of landscape. Destruction by color was very seductive to painters. Even the extremely orderly Braque painted magenta and pink seas, yellow and blue trees, but only for a time. Braque called it a "state of paroxism" (Elderfield, 1976, p. 141). For most painters, its extremism proved impossible to maintain.

Only Matisse, steady in his pursuit of an art of pure color and pure line, continued.

Phase Two: Constructing With Color

What form does pure color and pure line take? This was as ill-structured a problem as Cubism's quest to present multiple viewpoints simultaneously. The products of Matisse's first solution, drawing with color, were ambiguous. The fragmented form of Madame Matisse was barely separable from the stream beside which she sat.

The next *task constraint* precluded fragmentation, promoting (in its stead) unity, continuity. Matisse began to construct with color. Black contour lines, clearly separating things, were filled with unadulterated hues. Large, flat, patterned shapes no longer represented individual, specific things, but became signs of those things, types, icons.

Precluding the specific and the idiosyncratic further constrained color. In place of a multiplicity of hues, we see a dominant few. "Dance and Music" (1909–1910) have three: intense orange-red for the bodies, purplish-blue

[2]All dates for Matisse's paintings are taken from Schneider (1984).

FIGURE 4.2. From left to right, details drawn from "Landscape at Collioure" (1905), "La Conversation" (1908–1912), and "L'arbre de vie" (1949).

for the sky, malachite green for the grass. "The Red Studio" (1911) looks like its name: brick–red floods and flattens the walls, floor and furniture in the artist's studio. In "Conversation" (1908–1912), cobalt colors the garden pools, the walls, and the chair in which Madame Matisse sits; the green of the grass and trees is repeated in the collar of her robe.

Matisse's paintings from this middle period could easily become paint-by-number sets. You can see this in the center panel of our "Matisse" drawings (Figure 4.2), which shows just how simply the tree in "Conversation" is rendered. Of course Matisse continued to draw, not with paint, but with pen and black ink, concentrating on contour, on the rhythm of line alone. His late, great achievement was to draw without pen or brush. Henri Matisse picked up a pair of shears and, once again, changed his domain.

Phase Three: Cutting Out Color

The culminating *task constraints* were on traditional media, pen and ink, paint and brush. The late, large cutouts were "drawn" with scissors on sheets of colored paper (Cowart, Flam, Fourcade, & Neff, 1971). A single shearing movement linked pure line with pure color (the *goal constraint*).

The forms that resulted are truly iconic, symbols not for things, but for what those things can mean.

The paper maquette or model for "L'arbre de vie" (1949), a stained-glass window, is not a symbol for a tree, but for what a tree symbolizes—growth, renewal, life. A partial view of its patterning is shown in the right panel of our drawing trio (Figure 4.2). "The Tree of Life" (L'arbre de vie) is exuberantly colored. The leaf shapes are a deep Prussian blue; the flower shapes, a bright lemon yellow; the background, a warm cadmium green.

The amoeba-like shape that flowers on the tree multiplied and morphed into five differently colored flower-signs in "La Gerbe" (1953). Matisse also used it as a sign for other things that germinate and grow. In *Jazz* (1944), a book based on cut-and-pasted collages, it populates a lagoon, and stands for the heart of the woman at whom the knife-thrower aims his weapon.

The great simplifiers, it seems, are always great draftsmen, artists who can see the world as a single line. Picasso could see that way, and recognized Matisse as his only rival. Among more recent artists whose work I love, Matisse is the first chorus for Richard Diebenkorn's abstractions, both of brightly colored California landscapes, and of charcoaled or black-inked figures; for Ellsworth Kelly's elegant line drawings and shaped single-hued canvases.

Matisse is also in the first chorus of a young girl I met at the Brooklyn Museum of Art. She was with a group of children visiting the galleries, looking at and talking about angels' wings. Afterwards, in the studio, they all lay down on big sheets of brown paper and drew semi-circular wings (the kind you make in snow) with a black marker in each hand. The wings painted by this singularly gifted girl looked like the chasubles Matisse designed for the monks who said mass at the Chapel of the Rosary.

What Can We Learn From Matisse?

There's more than one way to change a domain more than once. Monet's involved changing his goal constraint, his question: How does light break up (a) on things, (b) between things, (c) alone? Matisse's way involved a *single goal constraint,* an unchanging question. His successive answers to "What is an art of pure color and pure line?" produced Fauvism and its metamorphosis from (a) color sketch to (b) colored blocks to (c) cut-out colors.

I think of Matisse's series of answers, his shifting *task constraints,* as approximations, as "sort of" criteria for his goal. The cutouts are the climax, the final criterion: *this* is what pure color and pure line look like.

A goal constraint, a question, as *generative* as Matisse's is rare. It gets a gold star for problem finding, for finding an ill-structured problem without a simple or single solution, a problem that can only be solved, re-solved, with a *series* of solutions.

Rothko and Abstract Expressionism

Rothko's *goal constraint* was never stated as clearly as Matisse's, nor developed as seamlessly as Monet's. It emerged as expressing tragedy, the tragedy of the time, the Depression, the War. Rothko first sought subjects, contemporary and archaic, that could evoke this emotion. Over time the goal, and the subject, became an abstract expressive form.

First Choruses

While Abstract Expressionism's name literally states its *task constraints* on representational and formal stylistic conventions, its practitioners, including its purest colorist, Mark Rothko, borrowed abundantly from the past.

Rotho's radically simplified compositions call to mind Matisse, who could make a black rectangle stand for an open door or window. His fluid shapes floating in fields of color recall late Monet. His palette reflects Bonnard's. Indeed, an alternate name suggested for the New York School was Abstract *Impressionism* (Ashton, 1998). Surrealism provided an early working method, automatic writing, and a subject—myth. There was an American first chorus too, philosophical as well as painterly. The philosophy was transcendentalism (think about Emerson and Thoreau), which exalted the sublime, a spiritual if not religious experience (Chave, 1989; Waldman, 1978). The painterly included Milton Avery's kind of minimalism, landscapes and portraits made with few, softly hued, flatly painted forms, and Arthur G. Dove's simplified, spreading organic shapes surrounded by haloes of modulated color.

Phase One: Constraining Realism

Realism, pictoralism, was precluded in a number of steps. All utilized Monet's *constraint* on motif, concentrating on single subjects. The first involved abstracting a real subject—passengers in New York City's subways; the second, abstracting an imaginary one—myth.

The stations in the 1930s[3] subway series are flattened, stylized spaces in which movement and interaction are suspended. Those who wait are separate, separated. The paintings are small and sad, sterile, expressive of emptiness. By the 1940s, the motif had become archaic, totemic. It was borrowed from Surrealism, along with automatic writing, a kind of doodling meant to elicit the irrational and the unconscious.

Rothko's first mythic subjects were Greek, his paintings deliberately indecipherable. There were two types of mythic paintings, exemplified by "Antigone" (c. 1941) and "Untitled" (1945). The figure of Agamemnon's daughter is beastial, with multiple heads, torsos and legs; those in the untitled painting are disembodied, a multiplicity of nondescriptive lines generated via automatic writing. Both paintings are composed in horizontal tiers—body parts in the former, colored bands in the latter.

The field neither understood, nor cared to understand the imagery. The mythic subject matter, like the earlier realistic one, would be constrained. As shown in Figure 4.3, only the horizontal bands of "Untitled" would be retained in "White Band," our preview painting from Rothko's second period.

Phase Two: Constraining Surrealism

Precluding Surrealism's insistence on imagery promoted a new concentration on color per se. Rothko's motif was now entirely abstract. He was painting light. The titles of many paintings from his classic period list their hues in parentheses: "No. 3 (Bright Blue, Brown, Dark Blue on Wine)" (1962), "No. 13 (White, Red on Yellow)" (1958), "Yellow and Blue (Yellow, Blue on Orange)" (1955).

As we saw with Monet and Matisse, constraints proliferate. *Task constraints* on composition followed the *subject constraint* on motif. The focus was the figure ground relationship. The backgrounds of the Surrealist paintings—the colored bands—morphed into figures. Color became form. At first multiplied and amorphous ("Multiform," 1948), Rothko's new figure-forms condensed, became fewer and rectangular, were stacked horizontally, sometimes with spaces between them. The rectangles were figure, the rest was ground. The true novelty was in how the figure and ground related, via contrasts and balances in all the attributes of light—hue, value, and saturation.

---

[3]All dates for Rothko's paintings are taken from Waldman (1978).

FIGURE 4.3. Formats for "Untitled," 1945 (left), and "White Band (Number 27),"
1954.

To allow the figure–forms to hang suspended over their grounds,
Rothko constrained paint application. Oils were applied like watercolors,
soaked into rather than stroked onto the canvas. Thin color washes were
laid one over the other. Rothko borrowed Bonnard's method of brushing
deeper hues over lighter ones to soften the edges of the rectangles, to make
them hover, resonate, appear luminous. Also appropriated was Bonnard's
palette, whose characteristic color combinations become Rothko's: blue,
purple, and brown; yellow, pinky–magenta, and green; orange, red, and
ochre (*Bonnard-Rothko,* 1997). These early combinations were vibrant, joy-
ful, expressive of ecstasy.

The spaces between the color forms can make them appear "mutually
attracted or dependent, at other times, barely touching, detached or es-
tranged" (Chave, 1989, p. 121). Formal properties—arrangement, color,
transparency, opacity—convey emotions. The rectangles, like Matisse's
cutouts, have become icons, equivalents for feelings.

Finally, so that the viewer would immediately and physically experience
the expressivity of his surfaces, Rothko, like late Monet, constrained the scale
and the height at which his paintings were hung. "Subway Scene" (1938) and
"Antigone" (1941) were only 3 feet by 4 feet and hung at eye level. "No. 61
(Brown, Blue, Brown on Blue)" (1961) was almost 8 feet by 10 feet and hung
so that the viewer's body coincided with the body of the painting.

Phase Three: Constraining Lightness

What Rothko called his "dark pictures" began in 1957 (Anfam & Mancusi-
Ungaro, 1997; Nodelman, 1998). This late series combines the initial and
revised *goal constraints*—the emotion to be expressed by the color forms is

once again tragic. Joy, transparency, lightness are precluded. Solemnity, opacity, darkness are promoted. The change appears in increasingly severe constraints on color and form that contrast both.

In the "Harvard murals" (1962), the rectangular figures are presented vertically instead of horizontally, joined at top and bottom, suggesting entrances to or exits from the dark plum background. An octagonal chapel in Texas houses the last paintings, a series of devastating austerity in which the soft edge becomes hard, the dynamic juxtaposition of hues becomes static, almost monochromatic. The theme of the Houston Chapel (1964–67) was the Passion of Christ. The paintings number 14, the same as the Stations of the Cross. Black and purple are the liturgical colors for death and mourning. Rothko likewise precluded all colors but two, black drawn in Figure 4.4, and—instead of purple—a red darkened to maroon. There are three triptychs, one reminiscent of traditional altar pieces. One is black washed with maroon. The other two have maroon fields and hard-edged rectangles. In their darknesses, the two hues no "longer seem to exist as physical color, but rather, as tranquil, tragic, twilit dreams of color" (Waldman, 1978, p. 68).

The effect is solemn, serious, existential, and in bitter contrast to the sensuousness of late Monet or the joyousness of late Matisse.

What Can We Learn From Rothko?

That early development may not predict late accomplishment. The early, myth-encumbered Rothkos are awful. The late luminous Rothkos are awesome.

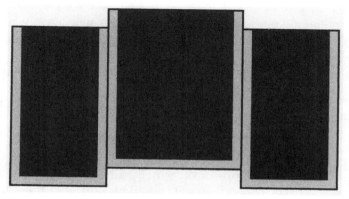

FIGURE 4.4. Side wall triptych, 1967.

This disjoint in development raises an interesting question: How did Rothko persist? Belonging to a group helped. Rothko's group is known as the New York School, or alternatively, the Abstract Expressionists. Its members shared his interests—some, like Still, Gottlieb, Baziotes, and Pollack were more involved in myth; others, including Motherwell and Gorky, in automatic writing (Russell, 1981).

They also shared *goal constraints*—all precluded representation, illustration, and promoted abstraction, expressive abstraction. They emphasized the act of painting, the painting as an object, a physically imposing object. They served as a sounding board, a support group. Ultimately each developed a "signature style" based on a set of personal *task constraints*—Pollack's slashed and dripped skeins, Gottlieb's sunbursts, Motherwell's elegies, Rothko's floating rectangular forms (Rose, 1986). Strangely, a signature style seems to mark the end of development, the closure of a constraint series. For most of the Abstract Expressionists, including Rothko, a signature style was a sign saying "No Exit."

Why? One could blame gatekeepers. Like the rest of us, critics, collectors, and curators are most comfortable with what they already know, what they readily recognize, what can be easily evaluated because goal criteria already exist ("Oh, what a *good* Rothko!"). Interestingly, this suggests that there is a different set of criteria for new and for established artists. Newcomers are expected to be producing novelties, experts, to be reproducing oldies.

Remember, too, that most behaviors are reliable, *slightly* different from what has been successful in the past. Few artists remain as variable as Monet or Matisse. Only two of the original Abstract Expressionists (Guston and de Kooning) abandoned their signature styles. De Kooning did it very late, like Monet. Also like Monet, his new, greatly simplified style was attributed to disability (dementia for de Kooning, cataracts for Monet).

The most important lesson to be learned from Rothko may be that even great creators can get stuck in successful solutions.

CONSTRAINING METHOD: MULTIPLES

Monet left many first choruses on which painters are yet improvising. Matisse was very clear about his debt to, and his difference from, Monet:

Each generation of artists views the production of the previous generation differently. The paintings of the impressionists, constructed with
pure colors, made the next generation see that those colors, if they can be
used to describe objects or natural phenomena, contain within them, independently of the objects they serve to express, the power to affect the
feelings of those who look on them (Flam, 1995, p. 196).

Rothko would no doubt have agreed.

Other artists took different things from Monet. In this section we focus
on working in multiples, a highly generative *task constraint* for producing
novelty.

Play it Again, Claude, Paul, Pablo . . .

For most painters, the purpose of this constraint is to force themselves to
see differently. Given enough skill, and a high enough variability level,
painting the same subject pushes the painter to someplace new. As we already know, for Monet, the goal was to see light differently. Here, "multiple"
meant a series of many paintings, of the same motif, at different times.

The Impressionist master was the first series painter. His series involved a *recognizable motif seen at separate moments,* at different times of
day, in different lighting conditions, in different seasons. To really know the
sea, he said—he could have added the haystacks, the water lilies—"you
have to see her every day, at all hours and from the same point of vantage"
(Patin, 1993, p. 153). As we've seen, he painted the grainstacks 23 times,
the poplars 24, the façade of Rouen Cathedral 27 times.

Cezanne, too, sat in front of a large, immovable object—a mountain, in
fact. Mont Sainte-Victoire is seen, like the cathedral at Rouen, at different
times, and painted multiple times, but to a different end. Cezanne wanted
not to record his sensations, but to organize and structure them, to "make
out of Impressionism something solid and durable" (Rewald, 1986, p. 159).
Monet's cathedral dissolves into small touches of color; Cezanne's mountain
is constructed with them. Cezanne famously said that Monet was "only an
eye" (p. 155). Indeed, while Monet sat in his garden and looked and
looked—at the Japanese bridge; at the iris bed; at the lilies, Cezanne constructed and reconstructed his still lives, making *multiple arrangements of
the same objects* that become separate pictures with different balances and
harmonies of color.

My Cezanne simplifications (Figure 4.5) show two still–life arrangements with the same olive jar, ginger– and sugar–pots, platter of apples, and

FIGURE 4.5. Partial views, "Still Life with Olive Jar, Ginger Pot, Rum Bottle, Sugar Pot, Blue Rug and Apples" (left, 1893–94), and "Still Life on a Table" (right, 1893–87).

a white cloth with a red band. The artist also painted *multiple viewpoints* of those objects in the same picture. Look closely at the drawing on the right. The olive jar is seen from above, the bottom of the platter from below, the sugar–pot from eye level. The Cubists built on one of Cezanne's approaches to the multiple. As we've already seen, Picasso and Braque painted *multiple viewpoints* within the same painting—but the views are of the same, not necessarily or easily recognizable, object or objects.

Another Cubist painter, Juan Gris, painted a platter with pears, also on a multiply folded cloth, from four perspectives. In my drawing of Gris's painting (Figure 4.6), the darkly outlined areas indicate the multiple views of the platter.

Multiple Choices: Contemporaries

Jennifer Bartlett makes productive use of another Cezanne strategy—painting *multiple views* of the same set of objects. In Italy, in 1975–76, Bartlett made 200 views on paper of a small garden with a pool, a statue, and a strand of cypress trees using different media (pencil, pen and ink, charcoal, pastel, watercolor, gouche) and different styles. John Russell (1982) called it an "encyclopedia" (p. 7) of a scene. To me, it is Bartlett improvising with great brio her way through the first chorus of Western art. The scene is presented and re-presented in classical perspective and Cubist planes, with Orphist color and Expressionist distortion. She makes me want to see all the ways that she can see.

She also, like Cezanne, makes *multiple arrangements* of the same group of objects. In "Rhapsody" (1975–76) a small set of motifs (cloud and mountain, house and tree, lines in different orientations, three geometric shapes) are

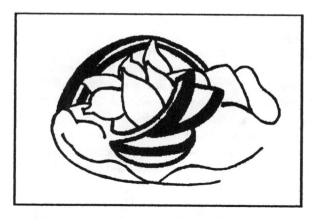

FIGURE 4.6. Detail from "Pears and Grapes on a Table" (1913).

elaborated, repeated, inverted, transposed on 1000 square enameled plates, using 25 colors. The mountain is altered in size, presented photographically, in outline, painted realistically or abstractly. The circle, square and triangle shift positions and sizes according to a plan that specifies the form and its size for a particular plate. For example, the left side of Figure 4.7 contains a large square, a medium triangle, and a small circle; the right side differs only in the size of the circle, which is now medium.

I said before that multiples force artists to see things differently. Bartlett uses multiples to show us how differently the same things can be seen. Sol LeWitt, another contemporary, plans his geometric wall drawings and paintings in much the same way that Barlett planned "Rhapsody."

Jasper Johns makes *multiple versions* of overly familiar objects—targets, stenciled letters and numerals, the American flag—that force us to

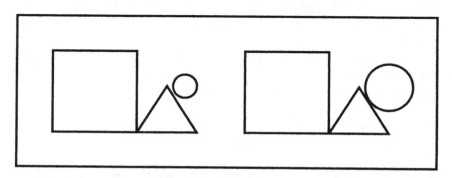

FIGURE 4.7. Panels from "Rhapsody" (1975–76).

actively see, rather than merely recognize them. He also paints and prints multiple arrangements of the same still–life objects—a Savaran Coffee can filled with paint brushes, Ballantine Ale cans, colored crosshatches.

We can't talk about multiples without mentioning an artist who famously, notoriously, used multiples not to see differently, but to emphasize sameness. You don't actually have to see an Andy Warhol to know what it looks like—a Brillo box, a Campbell Soup can, Che Guevera. Warhol's works are clearly separate in intent and intensity from his predecessors. Think of the multi-paneled portrait of Marilyn Monroe with chartreuse lips. What Warhol presents are *multiple views of nearly duplicated objects*. Multiple here means painting or printing the same thing in the same or almost the same way. There is nothing new to be seen, no new way of seeing it. This is Pop, ironic, aggressively appropriating the repetition and reproduction techniques of the mass media. All we can do is recognize the object, which is exactly what Monet, Cezanne, the Cubists, Bartlett, and Johns worked and work so hard against.

What Else Can We Learn From Monet?

The same thing that Cezanne, Gris, Bartlett, Johns, and Warhol (in his quite different way) did—that looking at the same object over and over again forces you—and also allows you—to see it differently. *Forces* you because your discrimination becomes finer; you notice things you didn't see the first or second or even the third time. *Allows* because no one painting or drawing becomes precious.

If you plan to paint the same four poplars all summer, you have all summer to figure it out, to try different things out. You can look at the poplars over and over. You can also look at what you've done and paint variations of it. Jasper Johns says he works this way. He says he takes an object and does something to it, and then does something else to it, and then something else (Castelman, 1986).

Never underestimate the power of a single scene, a solo still life. Multiplied into many works (like Bartlett) or multiplied in a single work (like Warhol), it can change the way an artist—and an audience—see the world.

A CONVERSATION: RHYTHM FROM REPETITION

To show that I practice what I preach, I'm using my own work as an example of a not-well-known painter using constraints to generate novelties. That makes this section a conversation with myself, a monologue of sorts.

My first obvious contact with constraints (not so-called, but constraints nonetheless) came in graduate school, at Pratt. Remember the dominant domain criteria for representational painting in Monet's day?—Contrasting values. If you get the darks and lights right, the result is a convincing illusion of three-dimensional space. At Pratt, we had to be able to do everything, and I wasn't getting the lights and darks exactly right. So my advisor, a painter named Ralph Wickiser (to whom I am ever–grateful) came up with the perfect combination of *task constraints*. One was Monet's constraint on motif. The others were Dr. Wickiser's. One constrained hue, this precluded contrasting color, and promoted contrasts in value. The other constrained value, the contrasts were limited to three—dark, medium, and light.

I stretched 10 small canvases (10 inches by 10 inches) and drew the same cartoon (a piece of driftwood) on each one. I prepared three values of one hue: dark, medium, and light raw umber. On Monday mornings, Dr. Wickiser would come to my studio (graduate students got small studios—mine had a window!) and put an "X" on a different part of each canvas, saying, "The light falls here . . . here . . . and here." I had no idea what he was talking about (I felt like Rapunzel with all that straw), but I had to paint all ten by Friday when he would come back, consider each, perhaps take one out and say, "This works, see you Monday."

It went on for three months. By the end of the first month, there were at least two that made each Friday's cut. By the end of the second month I was starting to see the problem, if not the solution. By the end of the third month I could squint and the world turned into three values. The *subject* and *task constraints* on motif and color made me see differently.

Of course, now, I have to come up with my own *task constraints*. The solution I get stuck in is, ironically, the result of that three-value constraint: my paintings tend to look like blown-up, close-up photographs. What I wanted to do was replace photorealism (a stylistic constraint) with something else. The problem was *what* else?

To find a new solution path, I painted several small, six-paneled screens (a constraint on format) with tempera (a constraint on media). I used a cartoon from a painting I'd done of parrot tulips. To spread it out over the six panels, I duplicated the shapes, but not completely. One of the screens looked like the drawing in Figure 4.8. If you focus on the second panel from each end, you'll see that they only partially repeat the blossoms from the central panels. I liked the duplication and tried the panel format

FIGURE 4.8. Folded screen.

in a flat oil painting (Figure 4.9). The tulips were orange with green and yellow markings. Without the folding of the screen, it was too busy (remember the *cognitive constraint*), so I painted over one panel in flat yellow, which helped make the composition even more abstract. That is, the rhythmic patterning precluded the photorealism.

I think of this current *task constraint* as a version of Monet's multiple, a single motif repeated in the same painting, sometimes with shifts in scale. In the third drawing (Figure 4.10), you'll see that parts of the tulips (wine-dark red this time), vase, and leaves are repeated in the two side panels. It's easiest to see the repeats if you look along the bottom.

For me, for now, abstract pure-color panels and patterning via repetition preclude photorealism and promote what the French call *decoration*,

FIGURE 4.9. Oil painting with solid panel.

FIGURE 4.10. Three–panel oil painting.

painting based on the relationship of the pictorial, painterly, elements (Watkins, 2001).

WHAT HAVE WE LEARNED?

How far can constraints structure and solve the creativity problem in art? As in literature, it depends on the *goal constraint* of the painter. The realization of a novel goal constraint can influence and expand a domain. This occurred in the cases of Monet, Matisse, and Mark Rothko, as well as with our earlier examples, Braque and Picasso.

Creativity is also possible working within a domain. As shown in the adoption and adaptation of Monet's method of painting multiples by his contemporaries (Cezanne, the Cubists) and ours (Bartlett, Johns, Warhol), the use of existing *task constraints* can generate great novelty and surprise. *Task constraints,* on a far smaller scale than Monet's, certainly, can even structure the creativity problem for a part-time painter like me.

CHAPTER 5

Constraints for Creativity in Fashion

What can we learn from Chanel? What can we learn from Schiaparelli? What can we learn from Rykiel? What can we learn from Kawakubo? What can we learn from Adrian?

What constraints structure the creativity problem in fashion? The verb "fashion" means to make. Clothing is fashioned to meet multiple *functional constraints:* protection, seduction, comfort, concealment, attention, ritual, rank. The noun "fashion," too, has multiple referents and attendant constraints: what kinds of things are made, how they are made, and which of them is *au courant*—in fashion.

Au courant is critical, reflecting fluidity not only in styles but more basically in kinds of "wears"—women's wear, men's wear, leisure wear, evening wear. What do you wear? What did your mother wear? It depends on whether you work—in the home, in an office, outside—and on what you work or play at, or work out at, for that matter.

In fashion, as in architecture, *formal (stylistic) constraints* follow functional ones.

Form, in turn, takes one of two paths. The first is discrete, rational, classic, Apollonian. It provides comfort, accompanies rite, confers and confirms status. The second path is outrageous, impulsive, convulsive, Dionysian. Its domain is spectacle, seduction, fun. The paths can cross, but one always dominates, as will be demonstrated in the first part of this chapter, which starts by showing how functional constraints influenced the fashions of Gabrielle Chanel and Elsa Schiaparelli. It continues by examining Chanel and Schiaparelli's continuing influences on two contemporary designers.

The second part of the chapter focuses on *subject constraints*. The subjects are characters, roles; the fashions are costumes. But first . . .

THE TWO PATHS: A DIGRESSION

Think about the old guessing game, the one with questions like "if *X* was a color, what color would it be?" If *X* was Chanel, the color would be beige; if it was Schiaparelli, the color would be pink, and shocking. Chanel never made a spectacle of herself, Schiaparelli always did.

Their differences began where differences always begin, at the start. Like Wright and Corbusier, their *first choruses* were literally worlds apart. Chanel, an orphan, was raised in remote Aubazade, in a secluded convent school. Schiaparelli, a born aristocrat, shared the Palazzo Corsini in cosmopolitan Rome with a family that included an Orientalist and an astronomer.

> Schiaparelli's impeccable social credentials gave her instant entrée into the high society that largely rejected Chanel. . . . [Her] innate sense of worth provided a firm base from which to rebel and to be deliberately frivolous. By contrast, Chanel who had to work and fight so hard and so long, could only be serious (Steele, 1991, p. 66).

Chanel, the *parvenu,* took the Apollonian path to redefine status; Schiaparelli used the Dionysian to flaunt it. As we shall see, their joint influences on fashion have not yet been exhausted.

FUNCTIONAL CONSTRAINTS: LIFE–"STYLES"

During the first 20 years of the 20th century, the statuesque, substantial Belle Epoque silhouette—ornamented and corseted into a rigid S-shape (defined by thrust-out bosom and buttocks) that impeded movement, signaling the leisured status of its wearer—collapsed into a handful of soft, drape-able, move-able cotton jersey or silk that served to conceal as well as reveal status.

Everything loosened up. Colors brightened, materials lightened. Dresses fell from the shoulders into shapeless, shortened tubes. Waists were no longer well-defined. Stiff, high collars relaxed into vee- and boatnecks; tightly fitted sleeves softened into fluid kimono, raglan, and dolman styles (Ewing, 1985/1992; Peacock, 1993). What were women doing that instigated the shift?

The principal occupation of the pre-World War I upper-class woman wearing Worth appears to have been changing costumes—from morning to day to tea to dinner to evening dress. In 1914, men went to war and women went to work. Work imposed new *functional constraints*; clothing had to allow free movement, had to hide dirt.

> Social events had to be postponed for more pressing engagements, such as caring for the wounded. Women donned nurses' uniforms or wore trousers in the arms factories . . . darker colors became the norm. Inevitably, by 1915, skirts rose above the ankle, and then to mid-calf (Baudot, 1999, p. 60).

The war ended. Royalty relinquished their crowns; women, their corsets. Androgeny was fashionable. Its symbol was the *garçonne,* the tomboy, or, better, the "bachelor girl." The term was taken from the title of a 1922 Victor Marquette novel, whose heroine cuts her hair short and wears jackets and ties—just like an independent *garçon* (Mendes & de la Haye, 1999).

Chanel and Poor Chic

Coco Chanel was an authentic *garçonne* who, born poor, made herself independently rich with, at least at the start, some help from her male friends. The help took two forms: cash to open her first boutique at Deauville, and her "first chorus" of masculine clothing (Scotch tweeds, short hair, sailor's jackets, white collars, cardigan sweaters, neckties, cuff links, knit pullovers) that she borrowed for women. The borrowing involved—no surprise—status as well as style.

The chic kept woman, wife or mistress, was still recognized by the conspicuous opulence of her costumes; her powerful protector by the casual simplicity of his. Costume is the appropriate word for what the kept woman wore. Chanel referred to it when she famously said, "Sheherazade is easy. A little black dress is difficult" (Steele, 1991, p. 44). What was Sheherazade? The Oriental costumes designed by Bakst for Diagaliev's Ballet Russes; their fanciful progeny in couturier Paul Poiret's pantaloons, turbans, and exotic gowns with names like Salome.

Chanel precluded the costume and promoted the casual, her kind of casual, which was called *poor chic*. The little black dress—the epitome of poor chic—was her answer to the overly fanciful or ornate, and to social snobbery. Chanel was not to the manor born, so she re-invented the manner. Her styles fit her lifestyle. She was independent, athletic, alluring; a businesswoman, a sportswomen, a very social woman who danced and dined with very rich men and very young men.

She proved extremely successful because poor chic proved not only elegant, but also supremely functional. The original little black dress, Figure 5.1, was a tube of wool knit. It had a bloused boat-necked top and a knee-length tubular skirt. The American edition of *Vogue* illustrated the dress in its May 1926 issue, predicting—correctly—that it would become a "uniform for all women of taste" (Edelman, 1997, p. 13). Uniform indeed, but also meant to be personalized with oversized, Byzantine-inspired costume jewels.

Oversize is important. Costume jewelry had originally been made to look real. Chanel's "stones" flaunted their fakeness. "A woman's neck is not a safe" (Baudot, 1999, p. 80), declared Chanel, her lacquered wrist cuffs extravagantly decorated with chunks of colored glass, draping rows of fake pearls over sweater sets, little black dresses, black knit tops tucked into loose white linen trousers.

FIGURE 5.1. Chanel's little black dress, 1926.

Well-dressed clearly meant less-dressy, but hardly austere. Gilt chains brightened up the trademark quilted bag and the classic knit suit with its collarless, braided cardigan jacket (and the silk blouse that matched its lining). Woman are still carrying that bag, and still wearing that suit, along with Chanel's two-toned shoe (designed to make the foot appear smaller), boater hat, and, of course, Chanel No. 5.

No other house has stayed *au courant* as long as Chanel's. The little black dress reappears annually on Fifth Avenue.

Schiaparelli and Spectacular Chic

Aristocrats have always worked hard at entertaining themselves and others. Dress designing for Schiaparelli was not so much a profession as an art (Baudot, 1997), an acceptable life-style, an entertainment. Entertainment too is a *functional constraint*. Like the artists whose company she kept—the Surrealists Dali and Cocteau, a quite different *first chorus* from Chanel's—she was drawn to extremes, eccentricities, and rapidly passing fancies. Her collections had themes: musical instruments, astrology, butterflies, circus, harlequins, cash-and-carry (the last featured oversized pockets).

Her first design caused a sensation. She put Surrealism into a sweater: fitted, black, with a tromp-l'oeil white bow knit across the front. Things were not what they seemed, or where they belonged.

In Surrealism, objects are displaced or dysfunctional. (Think about Magritte's paintings: A broken windowpane on the floor carries fragments of the landscape seen beyond the window; a mirror "reflects" the back of the person facing it.) Schiaparelli's displaced lips and hands were decorative and decadent. Appliquéed lips, in a high-keyed "shocking" pink, edged the pockets of a black tailored suit with broad, padded shoulders and a cinched waist. The famous torn dress ensemble—designed with Dali—paired a shawl with appliquéed flaps of material over a dress with slashes printed on the fabric. Garments became canvases, surfaces for elaborate or whimsical embroideries and sculptures: A pair of Baroque mirrors adorned the breasts of a black velvet jacket; buttons shaped like acrobats cavorted up a pink "circus" jacket with rows of plumed blue ponies. An embroidered hand (designed by Cocteau) rested on the waist of a gray linen dress (Martin, 1987).

The cut of a Schiaparelli suit was constrained by a current *stylistic constraint,* the sculpted '30s silhouette, which emphasized the waist and shoulders. In this suit from 1933 (Figure 5.2), the shoulders were not only emphasized, they grew "wings." Accessories, too, were transformed. Here,

FIGURE 5.2. Schiaparelli's winged suit, 1933.

entertainment was everything. Gold, claw-like nails grew on the fingers of black suede gloves. A sexy, high-heeled shoe metamorphosized into a hat (another Dali collaboration), impertinent and independent of any foot. The bottle of her perfume was modeled on Mae West's famous frontage.

Shocking, extravagant, spectacle as lifestyle is always a splinter movement, always a luxury, and always at risk. *Après moi,* said the Sun King— bewigged and bedazzling in gold brocade—*le deluge.* The deluge brought unembellished cottons in its wake. After the Second World War, Elsa Schiaparelli closed her Paris atelier; Coco Chanel reopened hers.

What Can We Learn From Chanel and Schiaparelli?

How *functional constraints* determine formal ones. How *formal, stylistic, constraints* fall in two categories: the classicism of Chanel, the flamboyance of Schiaparelli. Given the choice, whose clothes would you choose? What does your choice say about functional constraints in your life?

What else can we learn? That the timeless and the trendy may not be diametrically opposed. Anyone could make a spectacle of herself in a Chanel. In the next section, we'll see how creatively the two can be combined.

THE TWO PATHS: A CONTINUATION

Classic, easy-to-wear, and fantastic, look-at-me, looks continue as distinct design paths that are mixed, sometimes more subtly than a quick glance would discern. Contemporary designers who mix and match use the *functional* and *formal constraints* introduced by Chanel and Schiaparelli to generate novelty.

Sonia Rykiel: Mostly Classic?

"Clothing is like a memory. It summons up things from the past," Sonia Rykiel once said (Mauries, 1998, p. 12). Her memory is very selective, focusing closely on Chanel. How closely? Is the softly draped, white-collared ensemble (Figure 5.3) a Chanel or a Rykiel?

If anything gives away the answer, it's the missing rows of pearls that Chanel would have draped over it. But the constraints are the same: The criteria are comfort, casualness, elegance; clothes that fit the designer's lifestyle. Like Chanel, Rykiel has her way with knits, draping cardigans, skirts and sweaters into fluid, elongated lines.

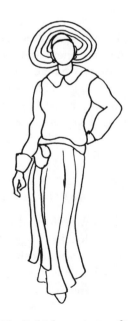

FIGURE 5.3. Rykiel sweater outfit, 1987–88.

Rykiel also shares the classicist conviction that designs should be basic, perennial standards to be worn for years. Thus, like the minimally updated and ever up-to-date Chanel suit, Rykiel offers not new looks, but what she calls *adjustments.*

The adjustments often add up to Rykiels that are obviously not Chanels. In 1974 the designer introduced clothes that showed off their structure, sweaters that could be worn inside-out. Rykiel said, "I showed that the other side of the garment, the part that touches the skin, the inside, was more beautiful because it was outlined with seams that resemble the vaults of a cathedral" (Maurias, 1998, p. 15). The outside seams are subtle, soft. Other adjustments are bolder, brassier: A gold lurex snake winds up an arm, lips are knit at the hip line of a shift. Both are on black. Belts have words writ large in rhinestones. Shades of Schiaparelli? Sort of, albeit in a playful, not theatrical or threatening way.

In the fall of 2002, in the window of Sonia Rykiel's boutique on Madison Avenue, I saw a black knit dress with a short, softly pleated skirt and a lipstick-red bow. The bow was gracefully placed, slightly off center, toward the right shoulder. Part of the bow (the part that bows) was real and tied. Part (the tails) were (like Schiaparelli's) tromp-l'oeil, knit into the sweater itself. Somewhat fantastic. Mostly classic.

Rei Kawakubo: Mostly Fantastic?

Like Schiaparelli, Kawakubo makes works of art to be worn. Also like Schiaparelli, Kawakubo works on surfaces—there is a famous ripped sweater, oversized and torn in apparently random places. However, the aesthethic is not the displacement of Surrealism, but rather the classic Japanese one of irregularity, asymmetry, imperfection—the surprising imperfection admired in Bizen-yaki, pots that emerge from the kiln with rough textures and "accidental" ash accents. My quote marks emphasize the accidental-on-purpose quality: the pots are fired for ten days, long enough for the fire and ash markings to accumulate. The rips in her sweaters are also accidental-on-purpose, produced by loosening some screws "here and there," says Kawakubo, in the knitting machines (Steele, 1991, p. 186).

Unlike and far more radically than Schiaparelli, Kawakubo resculpts the silhouette, challenging Western ideas of cut and fit. As shown in Figure 5.4, her first chorus is classic Japanese. The lines and layering of traditional clothing—loosely tied, quilted or block–printed, cut straight (think of Hiroshige prints, kimonos, yukatas, squared-off Samurai armor)—become the basis of oversized, abstract forms that wrap and twist or stand away

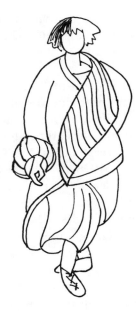

FIGURE 5.4. Kawakubo's oversized coat, 1984–85.

from and confound the shape of the body beneath. Her mannequins may wear the white makeup and kohl-black eyes of Japanese theater. She also uses Japan's traditionally somber palette to accentuate shape rather than surface.

Interestingly, the name of her company, *Comme les Garçons*, is reminiscent of Chanel's *garçonne* notoriety. Feminist connotations, like drawing attention to strength rather than sex, can be read into it. But I think it may even more directly refer to the unisexuality of classic Japanese clothing. At home, at any seaside resort, men and women still wear identical slash-sleeved yukatas, printed inside and out in indigo, brown, or black, tied with simple cotton sashes. Basically classic. Mostly fantastic.

What Can We Learn From Rykiel and Kawakubo?

How multiple first choruses create multiple, often unexpected, variations. Rykiel's Chanel-like softening of Schiaparelli's theatrics (the little black dress with the discrete red half-real, half-fake bow) make elegance electric. Kawakubo's exaggerated Japanese aesthetic creates both Kabuki–like (extravagant) and Noh–like (austere) costumes to be worn off-stage, theatrically. The lesson is to have a huge first chorus—to learn a lot, from lots of different people, lots of different places.

SUBJECT CONSTRAINTS: ROLE–"MODELS"

On stage, in film, roles serve as *subject constraints* which lead to *task constraints* on how a character is costumed. A well-designed costume conveys at first sight a character's social and economic status, occupation or aspiration, age, and most importantly, personality. It does this via exaggeration and simplification, confirming Oscar Wilde's observation that "All costumes are caricatures" (Russell, 1985, p. 5).

Costumes also do something else. Remember Calvino's thesis? We can neither recognize nor desire anything that we do not already know. The singular signature costumes designed for stars like Marlene Dietrich, Greta Garbo, and Joan Crawford provided models for the dreams—and the dress—of the Depression, and afterwards as well. The ultra-glamour of Dietrich, the enigma of Garbo, were the very stuff of fantasy. Crawford came closer to reality; her life story resembled her screen roles—social advancement through ambition and hard work. Her shoulder pads (precursors of power dressing decades later) signified a new and newly glamorous role-model: the self-made woman.

Fashions for Reel . . .

Signature styles showcased specific body parts (*functional* and *form-al constraints*) that symbolized the role each star modeled. Crawford's wide shoulders were synonymous with strength; Garbo's guarded face, with mystery; Dietrich's dramatic legs, with sensuality. Adrian Gilbert, the head designer at MGM, an expert at exaggeration and simplification—and glamour—dressed Crawford and Garbo; at Paramount, Travis Banton dressed Dietrich.[1]

What Adrian emphasized for Crawford was her already Tarzan-sized shoulders. He replaced her early bows and frills with sophisticated, almost architectural tailoring. The Adrian/Crawford shoulder-padded silhouette became the dominant style of the '30s and '40s. Ironically, Crawford's most famous padded-shoulder costume—the *Letty Lynton* (1932) dress—was frilly. As drawn in Figure 5.5, it was made of chiffon, white, starched, and ruffled everywhere. Accordian-pleated chiffon trimmed the demure Peter-Pan collar, edged the short peplum, the long flared skirt, and most exaggeratedly, and importantly, the oversized puffed sleeves that framed Crawford's

---

[1]All movie information, including dates, is taken from Engelmeer & Engelmeer, 1997; Fox, 1995; Riva, 1992; Tapert, 1998.

FIGURE 5.5. Joan Crawford's costumes for *Letty Lynton* and *Mildred Pierce*.

face. Even when she switched studios, Crawford didn't switch styles. The exaggeratedly severe suits (Figure 5.5) Milo Anderson put her in for *Mildred Pierce* (1945) looked as if they were designed by Adrian.

For Garbo's signature look, Adrian adapted her personal and very practical wardrobe. Practical meant both comfortable and covering. Garbo hated her hair (too thin) and her neck (too fat). The turtleneck, worn primarily by jockeys prior to Garbo's popularization, covered her neck. Hats—cloches, berets, slouches with rolled brims—concealed her hair. Her trenchcoat hid everything else. Only her face showed. Adrian simply exaggerated everything. He raised her necklines with draped cowls, stand-away collars, heightened jewel necks. In "A Woman of Affairs" (1928), her trenchcoat became oversized. With its collar turned up and her slouch hat pulled down, the focus was on that fabulous, flawless face. Covering Garbo up made her sexier. In "Wild Orchids" (1929), Adrian put her in voluminous men's silk pajamas. A famous photo from the set of "The Single Standard" (also 1929) shows her draped in a huge man's bathrobe, topped by a white, brimmed captain's hat.

Just as Adrian adapted Garbo's personal style, Paramount's costume designer, Travis Banton, built on Dietrich's, with Dietrich. The masculine was also exaggerated, but for different ends, and in different ways. Dietrich minimized the breasts she didn't like by shifting the focus to what she did like—her legs (which Paramount insured for $1 million, in 1931). Men's clothing covered what was above her waist and emphasized what was below. She was already infamous for wearing tails with a top hat in "Blue Angel" (1929). Banton dressed her in them again in "Morocco" (1930). In "The Scarlet Empress" (1934), he dressed her in a tight-fitting hussar's uniform trimmed with ermine. Banton also slit her dresses and put her in lace-trimmed stockings ("The Devil is a Woman," 1944). He designed her off-screen wardrobe as well. His "Marlene Dietrich" slacks became classics, always in fashion.

... and for Real

Women are still wearing Dietrich's slacks (I bought a pair last year). By 1930, they were wearing what Garbo wore—berets, trenchcoats, turtlenecks became classics. In 1932, after the release of "Letty Lynton," 500,000 copies (not exact copies, but close enough) of Crawford's dress were sold in the Cinema Shop in Macy's (Herzog & Gaines, 1991, p. 75). Puffy-sleeve became ubiquitous. Other movie stars wore it. Butterick Patterns even made it available to women who couldn't afford to pay ($30 or more!) for a Cinema Shop version.

This was and is very important. Creativity, we said, connotes influence. In America, in the 1930s, influence in fashion shifted from Paris to Hollywood which was accompanied by the increase in affordable ready-to-wear clothing. During the Depression, women who could no longer afford made-to-order, and working women, who could just afford the ready-mades, wore the same fashions. This influence is still felt by women when they tie fur collars around their necks, wrap themselves in greatcoats, show their legs through strategically placed slits in long dresses.

At the beginning of this century, movie stars do not wield this same influence. This may reflect the fact that today's actors and actresses no longer play the same roles on- and off-screen. Other single-role stars—rock stars, soap opera stars, Princess Di before her death (how many copies were made of her puffed-sleeve wedding gown?)—have taken their places as role and fashion models.

What Can We Learn From Adrian?

How constraints help create a signature style. The French have a saying *tout es change, tout le meme chose,* the more things change, the more they stay the same. A signature style is always the same and always *au courant* because it constrains selections in all seasons. There are two constraints—the body and the role.

Begin with the body. Which is the best view? What are its assets? What should be spotlit, exaggerated, accentuated? Alternatively, what could be camouflaged, minimized? Look at the life. Consider the roles. What costumes do they call for? A signature style should sustain a single look across costume changes. (A good clue to your own signature style is an outfit that makes you feel comfortable and attractive.)

A CONVERSATION: INTERPRETING, RECONSTRUCTING

Movie stars may not influence fashion anymore, but movies do; enter the designer as interpreter. What gets interpreted is often a cinematic image. Ralph Lauren's safari season—pale colors, linens, African prints, multi-pocketed vests and jackets—was an interpretation of "Out of Africa." His '40s look—tailored, subtly structured with shoulders, neat little hats and gloves—was an interpretation of "Casablanca."

Used clothing (not of the hand-me-down kind) has lots of uses. The interpreter's primary *constraint* is *stylistic;* the safari look seemed as if it came out of Africa. Stylists ferret out (at antiques shops, at estate or museum sales) original pieces from the time and place of interest (for authentic, readily recognizable cuts and colors). The originals are updated to fit current *functional constraints*—going to the office isn't the same as going to the delta. *Material constraints,* determined by what is available to work with, change as well. Linen blends look and stay crisper than too–slouchy, too–wrinkly, real linens that today's servant-less woman would have to iron herself.

A recent much-interpreted style originated not in the movies, but in the thrift shops. Teenagers were putting together used, unmatched tops and bottoms, cheaply. Prada interpreted the thrift–shop look, expensively. The next step was less-pricey lines and stores (like the Gap) interpreting the interpreter.

Used clothing is used in a different way by Jana Starr (personal interview, June 29, 2001). I talked with Starr in her shop on East 80th Street in Manhattan. What she searches out, refurbishes, and reconstructs is high-end (definitely not thrift-shop) antique clothing, much of it sold to brides.

"Reconstruct" is Starr's word. It's not interpreting, she said, because that involves updating (with new materials, new undergarments, and so forth) antique styles. Reconstruction re-arranges actual antique materials in new ways. The material Starr uses most is hand-tatted lace from Victorian wedding gowns. While brides of ten or so years ago opted for the original lacy, high-collared, long-sleeved gowns, today's brides want to walk down the aisle in lacy, collarless and sleeveless ones.

The original lace in a Victorian gown was ordered when a girl–child was born. Since nobody knew how tall or wide the bride-to-be would be, it was made in standard pieces to be assembled and sized at the time of the wedding. The skirt was a single piece of lace with an adjustable opening for the waist. Skirt pieces were fan-shaped, shorter in front and longer in back (for the train). Since Victorians wore their dresses over supports that lifted the material, the lace was longer from waist to floor than the brides were.

That extra length is what makes Jana's respecting-the-material reconstructions possible. Her major *task constraint* is, in fact, the material itself. "I won't put scissors to intact lace. On my watch, I don't want anything to happen to it. All I do is totally reversible" (2001).

By themselves (without hoop, bustle, or crinoline), the original skirts drape decorously from bra line to floor in front, and trail fluidly behind. Lace from the original tops (with the high collars and long sleeves removed) is fashioned into the sleeveless ones from which the gossamer skirts now fall. A new floor-length silk slip fits underneath. Antique ribbons trim the confection. Figure 5.6 shows one of my favorites with the original high collar atop a halter.

FIGURE 5.6. Antique lace wedding gown, Jana Starr.

WHAT HAVE WE LEARNED?

Do constraints structure the creativity problem in fashion? Definitely. *Function* is the primary constraint—clothing is worn for specific purposes. As purposes change (women's work, everyone's leisure), fashions change with them. *Formal* (casual, modest, regal, revealing) and *task constraints* (fabric, fabrication) determine how the functions are met. Influential creativity in fashion (Chanel, Schiaparelli) is facilitated when functional constraints change, allowing designers to expand the domain.

In turn, an expanded, flexible domain facilitates generative creativity. Rykiel's elegance, Kawakubo's extravagance (paralleled by the classic Garbo and the flamboyant Deitrich looks) were created within, generated by the *first choruses* created by Chanel and Schiaparelli.

While creativity is involved in interpreting and reconstructing, the difference from original design is significant. Designers transform their first choruses, interpreters translate theirs. It's useful to update the out-of-date. And importantly, reconstruction, like interpretation, can beget beautiful novelties.

CHAPTER 6

Constraints for Creativity in Architecture

What can we learn from Wright? What can we learn from Corbusier? What can we learn from Aalto? What can we learn from Pei? What can we learn from Gehry? What can we learn from Libeskind?

What constraints structure the creativity problem in architecture? Louis Sullivan's famous dictum "Form follows function" implies three constraints. Function, like motif, is a *subject constraint,* synonymous with the use to which a structure is put (to house people, paintings, offices). Form or style is a *goal constraint,* realized via *task constraints* on method (how the architect works), material (building stuffs and how they are put together), and site.

This chapter starts with three architects who pursued the same goal constraint, defining the shape or style that "modern" architecture would take. (This meant, of course, precluding the currently prevailing shapes.) Each devised a radically different solution path, developing a *series of constraints,* as well as a set of working elements or types to be refined, expanded, recombined.

The chapter continues on to museums—structures with a common *functional constraint,* housing and presenting artifacts. This section will, by the way, nullify Sullivan's dictum: There are many possible forms for any function. There are also alternatives to the museum's traditional function as a container.

Finally, we have a conversation with an architect about a container for two people, the Selfish House.

STYLISTIC CONSTRAINTS: WHAT SHAPE SHOULD A MODERN ARCHITECTURE TAKE?

In the early 1900s, "modern" in architecture—like Cubism in painting—was a goal without a criterion for knowing if it had been attained. Three architects whose styles provided criteria were Frank Lloyd Wright, Charles Edouard Jeanneret (known as Le Corbusier, or Corbu), and, from the second generation of modernists, Alvar Aalto.

Architectural styles emerge from, are based on, sets of typical elements or type-forms (Curtis, 1996) organized in characteristic patterns typical and characteristic, that is, of the *stylistic constraints* imposed by the individual creator. The combinatorial richness of these sets determines the ease with which *functional constraints,* as well as changes in scale (from a small private dwelling, say, to a large public structure) can be met. As we shall see, the richness of each architect's set increased as novel constraints were added.

In researching Wright, Corbu, and Aalto, I was fascinated by a *material constraint,* reinforced concrete. Reinforced concrete made modern architecture possible. The possibility depended on solving the problem of weight (Richards, 1940).

The problem is basically this: Whenever weight is applied to a surface (like a floor), the top part of the surface is compressed and the bottom part stretched. Concrete resists the compression on top, steel resists the tension below. Their combination allows the weight of a building to be shifted from large, load-bearing walls to smaller interior supports (piers, columns) beyond which a floor could project or cantilever.

What Wright, Corbu, and Aalto did with this flexibility was influenced to a large degree by the *material constraints* that preceded it. In the United States, where building was based on wood, Wright precluded the straight-sided box, using reinforced concrete to promote plastic, organic forms. Around the Mediterranean, where buildings were made of mud, stucco, and concrete, Corbusier precluded their curved, sloping shapes, using reinforced concrete to make straight, machine-like forms. In the far north, where layering and wood provide warmth, Aalto incorporated natural textures and ancient forms to preclude the severe starkness of Corbusier's solution to the problem of form.

Frank Lloyd Wright and an Organic Architecture

First Choruses

As the historian James Ackerman pointed out, "every artist finds his own antiquity" (Curtis, 1996, p. 166). That antiquity is, of course, the first chorus on which an architect improvises. Wright's first chorus, which provided his initial *stylistic constraints,* was both antique and contemporary. There were important Japanese elements. From traditional Japanese buildings Wright borrowed elements that emphasized the horizontal: overhanging roofs and transoms, open spaces divided by sliding screens. From Japanese prints he absorbed "the gospel of elimination of the insignificant" (Blake, 1965, p. 68). From the Froebel blocks and games of his childhood, he acquired a susceptibility to form and pattern. Rectangular blocks were combined to construct furniture and buildings. In some games, paper was pleated and folded into complex shapes. Other games used spheres, cones and strings. "The smooth cardboard triangles and the maple blocks were the most important. All are in my fingers," the architect wrote, "to this day" (p. 19).

Aside from the straight-sided silhouette which he meant to preclude, there were American borrowings as well: the informal plans, balconies, and verandas of the Stick and Shingle styles, the porches, overhanging roofs, and hearths of the midwest. The only architect whose influence was acknowledged by Wright was Louis Sullivan (of "form follows function"). The concept of ornament as organic, plastic, and continuous came from working with Sullivan, particularly on the Chicago Auditorium's (1887) intricate, interwoven natural forms. With Sullivan and his Art Nouveau predecessors, natural forms turned into highly stylized surface decorations. Wright would turn them into structural forms.

Goal Constraint

Wright's often–stated goal constraint was an *organic architecture,* which he articulated as—among other things—building from the inside out, making a unit of the building and its environment (Kaufman & Rayburn, 1965). To achieve this, Wright precluded separation, working as if a house were a single room, continuous with, but sheltered from, the outside.

Wright organized his type-forms (some structural, such as the cantilever and ribbon window, some functional, like the utility core and the carport) according to a grammar (his new *stylistic constraint*) developed around three *sub-goals*, horizontality, continuity, and plasticity (1965).

Sub-Goals and Type-Forms

Horizontality was a major sub-goal in both the Prairie (c. 1901) and Usonian houses (c. 1939).[1] The Prairie House was palatial, the equivalent of the servanted, upper–class European villa. The Usonian House was utilitarian, Wright's response to the social and economic consequences of the Depression. It was the prototype for the single-level ranch house, complete with dining nook, carport and deck.

Speaking about his own home, Taliesin, Wright said, "No home should ever be *on* any hill or *on* anything. It should be *of* the hill . . ." (p. 173). What if the home was not on a hill, but was on the Great Plains? How did Wright make a multistory house appear horizontal? By stratifying the layers of the building into horizontals that paralleled the flat site. The layers became the type-forms of the Prairie Style: cantilevers, overhanging roofs, ribbon windows, terraces or decks that extended into the landscape.

The cantilever, which worked like a "waiter's tray balanced on his hand at the center" (p. 201), was also critical to his second sub-goal, *continuity*. Continuity involved interpenetration of the interior spaces. By taking the structural load from the walls and placing it over a set of central supports, the cantilever allowed Wright to design with open, radial plans. *Open* meant that walls could become screens that defined or differentiated the public spaces of the house, while allowing them to slide past and flow freely into each other. The now popular Great Room was Wright's invention: He called it "the big room," and screened off areas for different uses. *Radial* meant rotating these semi-enclosed spaces in a pinwheel around the hearth of the Prairie House or the core of the Usonian House.

A typical Prairie floor plan has a cruciform shape, the two axes of the house intersecting at right angles and extending from the hearth. In my simplified sketch (Figure 6.1), the dark central block is the hearth, the dark area to the right is the carport.

A Usonian house, while smaller and L-shaped, also conforms to the open plan with a utility core. In the drawing (Figure 6.1), the smaller dark area is the core, consisting of back-to-back hearth and kitchen. The large dark rectangle is the carport. If you compare the Usonian and Prarie floor plans, you can see the shared side-step formation on the right of each. Wright was always interested in interesting spaces.

Continuity included inside and outside spaces, joined most dramatically in Fallingwater (1934–37). The site was not horizontal, but included

---

[1]All dates for Wright houses are from Kaufman & Rayburn (1965).

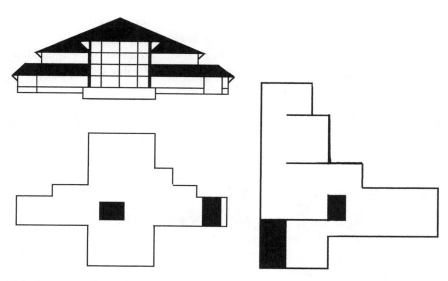

FIGURE 6.1. Left, schematic facade and first-floor plan of the Willitts House, 1902. Right, schematic first-floor plan of the Jacobs House, 1937.

both horizontal (the rock outcrops) and vertical (trees, cascading water) elements. To hold to his goal of an organic architecture, to make the house *of* the site, Wright now precluded pure horizontality, combining horizontal concrete cantilevered balconies with vertical stone walls and a massive stone fireplace. Spatial continuity was increased by dissolving the corners of the house (remember those freestanding, non-weight bearing walls) in glass.

The final sub-goal, *plasticity,* was related to continuity. It was initially realized in surface decoration that iterated, echoed, the shape of the building. For example, the decorative elements in Unity Church (1906) were linear and geometric, drawn in bands of flat trim that ran parallel to its supports (balcony, pulpit, column) and elaborated in dynamically arranged squares and rectangles. The interior looks surprisingly like Mondrian paintings from ten years later, and indeed, Mondrian's mature style (and the De Stijl movement to which it belonged) were highly influenced by Wright's work.

Plasticity was completely realized in the spiral form of Wright's last building, the Guggenheim Museum (1959). The type-forms that make up the Guggenheim—the central well, galleries overlooking the well, skylights, stairs outside the central mass—originated over 50 years earlier. They had been used in a rectangular form in the Larkin office building

(1902–06). A building of total continuity and plasticity had to wait until re-inforced concrete could be cast in a completely "organic" form.

Charting Wright's constraints (like charting Monet's) helped me iden-tify and articulate the continuities in his work (see Table 6.1). Like Monet in painting, everything Wright did became amplified over time. The Guggenheim is pure plasticity, pure continuity. And, like Monet's water lilies, the Guggenheim was the culmination of a continuously developing *series of constraints* that expanded, refined, and recombined an ever-growing set of type-forms organized in organic Wright-ian ways.

What Can We Learn From Wright?

The importance of a big, incompletely specified goal constraint. An *incom-pletely specified* goal constraint asks a question that hasn't yet been an-swered. Wright's question "What is an organic architecture?" was like Monet's question "How does light break up?"

A *big* incompletely specified goal constraint asks a question that can take a life's work to answer. The Nympheads were Monet's final answer to his question; the Guggenheim was Wright's. The life–work of each involved an evolving *series of sub-goals*, each of which helped define the ever-elusive

TABLE 6.1. Wright's Constraints

Goal	Sub-goals	Type-forms
An organic architecture		
	1. *Horizontality*	Preclude *interior-exterior separation*
		Promote *paralleling the site*
		→ cantilevers
		→ ribbon windows
		→ overhanging roofs
		→ terraces
	2. *Continuity*	Preclude *interior separation*
		Promote *open, radial plan*
		→ the big room
		→ screen walls
		→ utility core
	3. *Plasticity*	Preclude *surface-structure separation*
		Promote *paralleling the form*
		→ decoration restates structure
		→ pure spiral form

goal. Wright's organic architecture, in its developing definition, precluded separateness (a) between interior and exterior spaces, (b) between interior spaces, and (c) between surfaces and shapes.

Le Corbusier and Ideal Form

First Choruses

The *first chorus* that provided Corbusier's initial *stylistic constraints* was both more ancient and more modern than Wright's. The processional route of the Acropolis at Athens became a promenade through a building, revealing its form via the sequence of spaces. The much-admired systematic and ordered standardization of Roman buildings led to the Modular, Corbu's proportional system of measurement. Like Wright, he learned much from his early employers, acquiring a basic vocabulary for reinforced concrete buildings (exposed frames, pilotis or stilts, cantilevered upper floors, roof gardens) from Auguste Perret; an emphasis on functionalism and mathematical precision from Peter Brehems (Blake, 1966). The Cubist idea of simultaneously looking at the inside and the outside of an object is realized in three dimensions in Corbusier's interpenetrating exterior and interior spaces.

Goal Constraint

Not surprisingly, given his first (classic architecture) and continuing choruses (the machine-made, modern painting), Corbu defined achitecture as "the masterly, correct and magnificent play of masses brought together in light" (Le Corbusier, 1931/1986, p. 29). The masses to which he referred, the ideal forms, were "cubes, cones, spheres, cylinders or pyramids . . . the great primary forms which light reveals to advantage" (p. 29), realized in the anatomy of the ancient (the Temple of Luxor, the Parthenon), the machine-made (power stations, ocean liners), and in modern painting (Cubism, De Stijl).

His *goal constraint* was to order these masses, to arrange them rhythmically, according to a plan. Rhythm itself results from measurement. Again I quote from Le Corbusier (1931/1986): "Units of measurement are the first condition of all. The builder takes as its measure what is easiest and most constant, the tool he is least likely to lose; his pace, his foot, his elbow, his finger" (pp. 70–71). Corbusier wanted his basic units, his type-forms, to be standardized, mass-produced. His proportional system, the Modular, would provide the organizing grammar capable of generating an infinite number of variations within the unit system. The variations can be clustered around his two *stylistic sub-goals:* first, the *machine for living,* and later, the *deux-ieme era machiniste* (the second machine age), Corbu's constraint on his earlier pure machine aesthetic, his version of an organic architecture harmonizing industrial and natural forms.

Sub-Goals and Type-Forms

The *machine for living* was to be equivalent in elegance and efficacy to those other modern machines—the ocean liner, airplane, and auto—which resulted, the architect said, from a clear statement of the problem to be solved. For example, the airplane was possible once the goal changed from "flying like a bird" to "a flying machine with a means of suspension and propulsion in the air" (Le Corbusier, 1931/1986, p. 113). Likewise, the problem of the dwelling could be solved only when the standards, the criteria, were stated. For the dwelling, Corbusier listed three: It must provide functional spaces and shelter and be a receptacle for light and sun. He then asked, as Wright did, "Why the scanty windows with their little panes; why large houses with so many rooms locked up?" (p. 115).

Corbusier called his initial solution to the now properly stated problem the "Five Points of a New Architecture" (Curtis, 1996). The machine for living was to be built with the new *material constraint,* reinforced concrete, which by eliminating the load-bearing wall made possible Corbusier's five points or type-forms: pilotis, open plan, free façade, ribbon window, roof terrace. The basic element was the pilotis, or pillar, which lifted the building off the ground. Going back to his first chorus, the pilotis is the column of the Acropolis, now unadorned, unornamented. It is also the antithesis of Wright's binding a building to the horizon. The open plan, made possible by the pilotis, used partition walls to model the interior spaces, and to integrate them with, open them, to the outside. The Modular proportion system organized the interiors into interlocking spaces of at least two related (2:1) heights.

The prototype for this version of a new private dwelling was the Maison Citrohan of 1922.[2] The Maison, a white box on stilts, had a double level for the living room, a single level for the kitchen, bath, and bedroom, and two terraces, one halfway up, the other on the roof. The Villa Savoye (1928–31) was a more elaborate version, hollowed out with interior terraces,

---

[2]All dates for Corbusier houses are taken from Blake (1966).

and incorporating a grand promenade or architectural route along a ramp that rose inside between the ground and first floors, and outside from the interior terrace to the roof terrace.

The *second machine age* began with the Unite d'Habitation (1947–53), Corbu's prototype for collective housing. The Unite combined standardized factory-produced units into 23 different apartment layouts, each with the 2:1 ratio of the Maison Citrohan (a two-story living room backed by bedroom, bath, and kitchen on one story). It contained public as well as private spaces, including a children's pool, a gymnastic area for adults, and an open-air theatre on the roof.

The major difference between the earlier Villa Savoye and the Unite is in their facades: the Villa had a smooth, streamlined finish; the Unite, a rough, deliberately textured, pebbled surface. What this change reflected—an earthy, natural rather than mechanical emphasis—was Corbu's emerging interest in architectural vernaculars (folk forms like the Catalan vault). The result was not a totally new vocabulary or grammar, but an elaboration of the original five points. New type forms were introduced: *beton brut,* or bare concrete; *brise-soleil,* moveable grilles to block the sun; *aerateurs,* ventilating panels. Walls became thicker, rounded, in fact, more traditionally Mediterranean. Corbu now precluded his own initial constraints on form and finish.

The Chapel of Notre-Dame-du-Haut at Ronchamp (1950–51, see Figure 6.2) was, like the Guggenheim, a sculpture in the round. Was Corbusier becoming Wright?

Not exactly. While he did return to more organic forms, they became increasingly archaic, purposefully rough. Another strong formative difference was operating. Wright's first chorus was the prairie, where homes were few and far between, spread out and open. Corbu's was the Mediterranean village, with its buildings close, vertical, and enclosed for privacy. The

 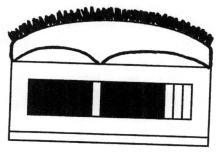

FIGURE 6.2. Left, schematic of Chapel of Notre-Dame-du-Haut. Right, schematic of Maisons Jaoel with concrete and grass roof.

Maisons Jaoel (1951–52, see Figure 6.2) exemplified this new, closed, archaic character. Deliberately crude, earth-hugging shelters with curved Catalan vaults and turf roots, they were characterized by an English architect, Peter Smithson, as being "on the edge of peasantism" (Curtis, 1996, p. 425).

What Can We Learn From Corbusier?

The importance of clearly stating the problem that's up for solution. A clear, complete statement of a building problem involves specifying *formal* (style or goal), *functional* (subject), and *task* (material) *constraints*, as well as criteria for knowing if the constraints have been satisfied. Corbu used constraint specification as a tool to structure his problem spaces.

Once specified, some of Corbusier's constraints remained constant (the modular system for proportions, the type-forms). The ones that changed (precluding his early streamlined finishes and promoting his late rough finishes) restated some, but not all, of the criteria for solution.

Alvar Aalto and the Naturalization of Modernism

First Choruses

Like Wright, Aalto was influenced by Japanese architecture. However, where Wright borrowed horizontal elements, Aalto adopted *moveable* ones, the sliding shoji screen or wooden door that partitioned, closed, or opened space. Like Corbusier, he was attracted to ancient Greece and to Cubism, but in different ways. Aalto focused on the fan-shape of the Greek theater; on Cubism's collage techniques and fragmentation of figure and ground.

Aalto's emphasis was on the biomechanical. From Corbusier's Five Points, he took prototypical modernist forms (the mechanical), altering them with uniquely Finnish elements (the biological). From the Finnish landscape, Aalto absorbed dynamic forms (undulating waves sculpted on the bedrock by glaciers, vertical forest rhythms) and natural materials (pale pine and birch woods; bound, woven, tied, and matted fibers); from Finnish architecture, he borrowed both archaic (the primitive hut) and vernacular (the farm fence enclosure) type-forms (Trencher, 1996).

Goal Constraint

Serendipitously, prophetically perhaps, "aalto" in Finnish means "wave." The wave form, an undulating curve, is prominent in Aalto's work, and representative of his overall goal constraint, the *naturalization of modernism*. The wave precludes the overly and overtly rational, and promotes a more romantic modernism, one attuned to natural (and, in his case, national) conditions. Our first two modernists attended to local conditions, but inconsistently: Wright in his early work, Corbusier in his later. Aalto did it always, and with the single-minded goal of bringing us closer to nature.

Sub-Goals and Type-Forms

Aalto's accomplishment was based on a synthesis of three stylistic sources, which served as sub-goals: *the ancient, the local,* and *the modern*. His type-forms followed from his sources (Trencher, 1996).

From the *ancient* came arch-types. Architectural arch-types express the basic forms of human society: Space is not conceived as an abstraction, but rather as an enclave with its connotations of belonging and safety. One such arch-type is the primal shelter, the primitive hut. Another is the harbor, also sheltered, surrounded on three sides. In Finland, the house-as-harbor appears in the expandable Karelian farmhouse, a group of structures forming a loosely defined three-sided enclosure, linked to its surroundings at different levels. This traditional opened-up courtyard was the basis of Aalto's (also expandable) L-plan. A third arch-type is the amphitheatre, set into a slope, gathering a community.

From the *local* came natural elements and traditional ways of working them: pale, bendable pine and birch woods; woven, tied, and twined reeds and grasses; the turf roof; the stick or stone fence. In the far north, wood and layering provide warmth. To the sere, stark whiteness of the south, Aalto also added natural forms, in particular the wave.

From the *modern* came the open plan and the technical means for constructing with undulating surfaces, fan-shaped volumes, movable walls.

Melding the ancient, the local, and the modern produced two additional constraints, which together define Aalto's style. The first (stylistic) constraint precluded rigidity and promoted *irregularity*. The second (task) constraint, *layering*—of structure, of space, of surface—produced the dynamic ordering and the rich textures of Aalto's buildings, for example, the early Villa Mairea (1938–41).[3]

The Villa, with its successive shifts in space and surface (irregularity and layering), clearly precludes the sparse, classic ordering of early modernism. The outside of the main "L" plan (bottom of Figure 6.3) provides a formal

---

[3]All dates for Aalto buildings are from Trencher (1996).

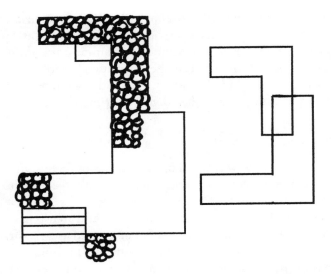

FIGURE 6.3. The left panel is a summary version of the plan for the Villa Mairea; the right shows how the two "L"s intersect.

public façade; the inside, a semi-enclosed private space. A subsidiary "L" structures the rear court with pool (not shown in Figure 6.3) and sauna (the smaller white rectangle). Together, the adjoining "L"s form an enclave (the ancient).

Aalto's original plan, like my simplified version, was textured, hinting at the series of structural layers, multiple half-levels (the modern) that increase in rusticity (the local) from the formal, geometric, white-walled entrance to the turf-roofed stone-and-stick sauna at the rear. The sauna is modeled on the primitive hut, here a specifically Finnish one, surrounded by huge stones (the ancient and the local).

The architect's studio and office (1955–62) provides another clear synthesis. The plan is a modified "L." The surprise is the shape of the now–expected enclave (the local). It is fan–shaped, provided with irregularly placed stone seats arranged in arcs, reminiscent of a small ruined, albeit Greek amphitheatre (the ancient).

The most innovative result of precluding rigidity was the moving wall. The wave as ceiling, undulating in wood (the modern and the local) above a long lecture room appeared with the Viipuri Library (1927–34). Rearrangeable bentwood stools provided seating under the waves. Moving walls in the Viipuri took the low-tech forms of lightweight folding screens and curtains. Aalto's highest-tech moving walls, magnifying the ritualized space (the ancient) of the Vuoksenniska Church (1956–59), are multi-ton, made of concrete, and stored in curved interior bays. The straight west wall reflects sound, the curved east walls diffuse it, the moving walls balance it.

Aalto's solution path was elegant, seamless. It also has the quality that I attribute to Braque's but not to Picasso's paintings, to Wright's but not to Corbusier's evolving series of constraints—inevitability, the result of a single-minded pursuit of an unchanging goal. Aalto also had the advantage of Wright and Corbusier as part of his first chorus. Both pushed the limits of current technology (reinforced concrete construction, the *material constraint*) for stylistic ends *(goal constraints)*. Both attended, although at different times in their careers, to the local, the organic, the natural.

What Can We Learn From Aalto?

Three things. First, that newness often involves *renewal*. In renewing traditional Finnish forms, Aalto reinvented, romanticized Corbusier's modern, primarily Mediterranean, ones. The converse also holds. In renewing modern forms, he reinvented traditional ones. The result was, importantly, an architecture that is *emotionally satisfying* as well as *efficient*. This is, itself, the second thing to be learned: meeting emotional needs can be highly functional.

Aalto's romantic improvisations remind me of Calvino's take on memory: We cannot desire nor be nostalgic for anything we do not already know. Aalto knew a lot. His first chorus was very rich. It rested, like all Romantic work, on a Classical foundation (provided in large part by Corbu). It resonated, like all Romantic work, with the archaic, the pre-classical. The third thing to be learned (or at least reminded of) is the importance of an extensive, extravagant, elaborate—and also emotional—first chorus.

FUNCTIONAL CONSTRAINTS: THE SHAPES THAT CONTAINERS TAKE

Museums are for holding (displaying, storing) stuff, collections of stuff, natural curiosities, artifacts, art. You can think of the museum as a container with lots of *constraints—functional* (subject), *stylistic* (goal), *material* (task). The size and shape the container takes traditionally depend on its contents, the style of the container on current styles for containers called museums, which in turn are constrained by the materials available for container construction.

The Classical Container

In the 19th century, museums were built to look like the beaux-art palaces that much of their contents (paintings, decorative arts, and so forth) were made for. These provide the *stylistic constraints* for what most of us think of as a classic, prototypical, museum. My favorite example (and my favorite museum) is the Metropolitan Museum of Art, in Manhattan. It's got all the classical type-forms: a central dome and grand staircase; enfilades (see Figure 6.4), or galleries lined up in perspective, rather like the Temples at Luxor; wainscoting and molded paneling (especially in the 19th century painting galleries); skylights for natural light (in the ancient art galleries, all the new wings—Lehman, Sacker, Rockefeller—and sculpture courts). The Met, too, has multi-form galleries designed to hold specific collections: a huge glass cage for the Temple of Dendur, darkened recesses for Islamic prayer rugs, a Federal period "house" for Americana.

The Modernist and Post-Modernist Container

Early 20th century modernism expanded the domain, opening up, and cleaning out, the classical container. Artificially lit, loft-like spaces with flat–white partition walls took the place of "articulated," decorated interiors. The container became neutral, reminiscent of no other place or time, capable of displaying any content. Thirty-some blocks down Fifth Avenue

FIGURE 6.4.   Enfilades provide processional space in the classic container.

from the Met is an early example, MOMA (1939, Philip Goodwin and Edward Durell Stone).[4] Across the continent, a more eclectic post-modern example, San Francisco's MOMA (1995, Mario Butta) includes and updates type-forms from the classical container: the sky-lit dome, grand staircase, and enfilades. The dome is translated into a 135–foot central cylinder; the monumental staircase is embellished with square balconies, and the second–floor galleries are symmetrical, sky-lit, and processional. The other floors are Cubist-modernist: fragmented, layered, with spaces of varying sizes and heights.

I am not exactly sure where IM Pei's breathtaking Miho Museum in Shiga, Japan (1997) fits. It is too elegant to be post-modern, too Japanese to be pure modern. Let us take as its theoretical precursor Aalto's romantic modernism, attuned (as we said) to natural and national conditions. The Miho has elements of traditional shrine architecture. It reminds me of Ise (the most important Shinto shrine in Japan). There is the distance to be traveled before arrival (an hour's drive from Kyoto), a ritualized passage (an underground tunnel, a footbridge over a ravine), and roofs that appear and disappear in a mountainous wood. Pei borrowed, too, the shape of the shrine roof (an isosceles triangle), replacing the old, overhanging reed thatch with glass and steel in geometries related to Mingei, or folk-art patterns. The entrance is a circle, which represents perfect harmony and beauty, the goal of the Shinji Shumeikai sect, to whom the collection and buildings belong (see Figure 6.5).

As arresting in its simplicity as the modernist, or in its overlays as the post-modernist, container becomes, it does not compete with its contents. The conspicuous container does.

The Conspicuous Container

The first and most famous example is the building we said we'd get back to, Frank Lloyd Wright's Guggenheim Museum (also on Fifth Avenue and closer to the Met than to the MOMA). The Guggenheim's spiral shape (see Figure 6.6) did more than realize Wright's ideas about plasticity and continuity; it presented an even more radical translation of the dome and grand staircase than the post-moderns which followed it. The dome became the grand central skylight that lights the whole space and not just the entry; the grand staircase became a ramp through the entire processional space that

---

[4]All dates for museums are taken from Donzel (1998) and Newhouse (1998).

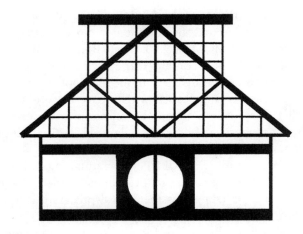

FIGURE 6.5. Simplified version of the entrance to the Miho Museum.

moves downward from the skylight, and provides multiple perspectives on the displayed contents.

The problem with the Guggenheim is that while its function is to be a container, its architect was *not constrained by function*. What Wright built is a gloriously expanding, exhilarating sculpture to walk through, rather than around. The artworks that it complements are also sculptures (Calder's mobiles hovering over the central core, David Smith's ironworks descending the ramps) or sculptural (Ellsworth Kelly's huge, shaped monochromatic canvases). In other cases, the container overwhelms its contents. (This is why there are additions, straight-walled galleries where the contents win.)

There is now another conspicuous container named Guggenheim. This one is at Bilbao, in Spain, and was built in 1996 by Frank Gehry, who, like Wright, reinterpreted the traditional dome and grand staircase in a new kind of grand style. Here the dome became a flower whose curved "petals" are cut out (like Matisse's) of shimmering titanium. The atrium under the petals is 1½ times the height of Wright's, and, like Wright's, curvilinear. The staircase is a series of catwalks, reflecting a Cubist, rather than a continuous-plastic criterion. The flower-tower is the core from which the multiform galleries (the largest is boat–shaped) extend (Newhouse, 1998).

This Guggenheim, too, competes with its contents. Despite the inclusion of different kinds of spaces to contain different kinds of content, Gehry's museum—like Wright's—best complements large, geometric, sculptural stuff (like Richard Serra's rust-colored metal ellipses or snakes).

FIGURE 6.6. Schematic façade of the Guggenheim Museum, New York.

The Content-Free Container?

Traditionally, museums have been identified with their collections; the two Guggenheims are identified with their architecture. Wright's building houses its permanent collection of early 20th century masterpieces in a small rectangular addition entered off the main ramp. Gehry's building only houses temporary exhibitions. Perhaps the lack of extensive, permanent content changes the *subject* or *functional constraint*. If the contents cannot be identified, the container will be.

An extremely dramatic example of this is the extension for Berlin's Jewish Museum (1998, Daniel Libeskind). The skylight and dome are replaced by a sky-lit 13–foot wide structural void that appears over and again in the zig-zagged exhibition spaces (see Figure 6.7).

There is nothing in the void except the narrow concrete bridges that span it. Slanting girders cross the space above the monumental main staircase. Oblique, too, are the asymmetric incisions that pass slices of light onto the gallery walls. The interior space is threatening, overwhelming. The museum has aptly been called "a monument of mourning" (Newhouse, 1998, p. 239)—a monument, *not* a container.

What Can We Learn From Containers?

How *functional constraints* can be stretched, sometimes to the point of subversion. The function of the building we call a museum is to contain (store, display) things. Classical, modern, and post-modern museums meet this constraint, using quite different *stylistic constraints*. The conspicuous

FIGURE 6.7. Floor plan of the Jewish Museum extension. The black space is the void.

container alters the constraint—proper display is limited to the large and the sculptural. The content-free container subverts the constraint entirely. The museum-as-monument meets, like Aalto's buildings, emotional needs. Unlike Aalto's buildings, its *primary* function is to meet emotional needs.

These changes in functional constraints underline the importance of Corbusier's tool—clearly stating a goal and the criteria for meeting it. Precluding some objects and promoting others are legitimate criteria. Sculpture parks, like Storm King Mountain, are open-air museums for large-scale and environmental pieces. Film and video museums resemble movie theatres (small, dark spaces, with seating) more than a classic promenade past unmoving objects. Calling an emotion-evoking object a museum (and not a sculpture) verges on misrepresentation.

A CONVERSATION: CONTAINERS FOR PEOPLE

The building with the function most familiar to us is the dwelling, the residential container for people. Residential containers differ in the numbers and needs of their residents, whether singles or single-families, multiple families, or multiple singles (the last in assisted living facilities, nursing homes, or hospitals). Dennis Kaczka (personal interview, September 8, 2001), an architect from Kinnelon, New Jersey, designs and constructs all kinds of residential containers. He talked with me about constraints common to all.

Goal Constraints

One goal constraint is *functional*—maximizing property use, getting the most building that site, code, and client constraints allow. The other is *stylistic* or aesthetic, and involves working, within a style appropriate to the site, the area, and the sensibility and skill of the architect. These constraints are addressed in a series that starts with site and ends with style. I've numbered the series in the order Kaczka gave them.

1. *Site constraints.* Dennis Kaczka called the piece of property on which a residential container is to be located the "site envelope." Configuration, topography, and size all serve as constraints on the building that a particular site will envelop.

2. *Code constraints.* The building, too, is called an envelope, one that contains its residents. Its size is constrained by building codes that specify "bulk requirements." These requirements are based on things such as setbacks and frontages, footprints of existing or former buildings, and population densities. Densities are based on building/property ratios. If a local ordinance allows four building units (of X size) per acre of land, then one acre might hold four separate houses, four attached townhouses, two low-rise or one medium-rise apartment houses. There are obviously more units in the medium-rise apartment than in the single-family house, but the ratio of unit to land is constant.

The number of allowed units also increases when personal spaces are shrunk and common spaces clustered. For example, when older adults move from single-family units to assisted living facilities, their apartments are smaller because kitchen, dining, storage, and recreational facilities are common spaces, combined, shared by all residents. When even older adults move to nursing homes, their personal spaces again shrink (to single or shared-room size) and common spaces expand (to include treatment facilities).

3. *Client constraints.* Only after site and code constraints are assessed can the architect address the individual client's *functional* constraints (what uses will this container have, how much money will be spent to build it) and *stylistic* constraints (what will it look like).

4. *Stylistic constraints.* When I asked Kaczka to describe his "signature," he mentioned a number of things. The primary one was "stylizing" traditional architecture. Stylizing has several senses. One is simplification. Ornamented with neither acanthus leaf nor scroll, a stylized column is simple, emphasizing outline rather than embellishment. Another is transformation. A traditional Cape Cod has one-and-a-half floors; the half-floor houses small, boxy upstairs bedrooms. In a stylized Cape Cod, the half-floor becomes a cathedral ceiling, an open loft.

A second, and related, constraint is selecting an indigenous (to the area) style for stylization. A third is a preference for asymmetry. A fourth is "framing what's outside," placing openings for their views, rather than simply punching windows in.

To see how these constraints affect an actual container for people, we looked at a particular house, a "selfish" house (his term), a lakefront house built for two adults who use it on weekends during the whole year and for weeks during the summer.

The Selfish House

Site and *code constraints* bound the house to its original footprint, to the same number of bedrooms (a density requirement), with limited capacity for expansion. *Client constraints* were relatively relaxed. Since the couple had spent many years in the to-be-replaced summer cottage, they wanted the new house to feel "familiar." Their *stylistic constraints* were to retain the basic layout and the feel of the screened–in porch that fronted the lake. Their *functional constraints* included adding studio space (painting and other projects had been done on the open porch), enlarging the kitchen and the bath space.

The architect's first *stylistic constraint* was selecting an indigenous style, a Cape Cod. What Kaczka designed was a Cape Cod that—although stylized—looks as if it had always been there. A traditional Cape Cod is symmetrical, with one and a half stories, a 12 x 12 foot pitched roof with no overhang, small windows, and clapboard or cedar siding. To "breathe space" into this kind of container, he changed the second boxy-bedroom story into a studio-loft overlooking a great room with a cathedral ceiling. In place of an attached staircase, the studio is reached via an open spiral. Instead of small windows, there are two huge oculi (round windows), continuous casement windows where the screened-in porch was, and paired windows at every corner, that frame panoramic views of the lake, lawn, and trees. Instead of a single roof line without an overhang, there are two levels, their symmetry offset by the chimney and an overhang (on one side) supported by very simplified columns.

My quite–rough drawings (Figure 6.8) show the floor plans of the summer cottage (left) and the new year-round house (right). In the plans, the thicker black areas on the outside walls indicate windows, the gray areas indicate doors. The spiral staircase leads to the studio loft above the kitchen.

The next two drawings (Figure 6.9) show one side of each house. Again the old house is on the left and the "selfish" house (with the very noticeable oculus) is on the right. The darkened areas indicate windows and doors.

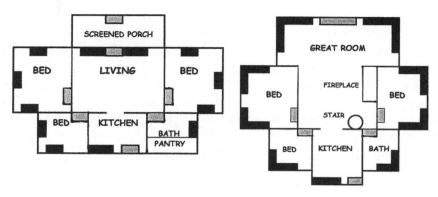

FIGURE 6.8. Floor plans of the old and new lake houses.

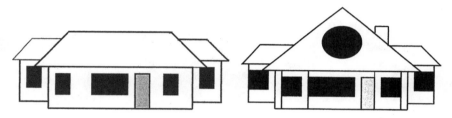

FIGURE 6.9. Outside views of the old and new lake houses.

WHAT HAVE WE LEARNED?

Do constraints structure the creativity problem in architecture? Yes, and at all levels.

How far? In some cases, very far. We've seen how different domain-enlarging *stylistic constraints* (Wright, Corbu, Aalto) can arise from a shared *goal constraint* (modernity) and/or a shared *material one* (reinforced concrete). Also how radically different structures (containers for things) can share common *functional constraints*. In some cases, structures meant to satisfy a functional constraint can confound (the conspicuous container) or even subvert it (the content-less container). And how containers for people can combine *stylistic* and *functional constraints* in highly personalized (by the architect, for the client) ways.

Also, not so far. Most buildings, in most cities, in most towns, in most of the country, are not built by architects. I first wrote "not designed" by architects, but that's not true. There probably was an architect (and probably more than one) behind every set of plans in a developer's or do-it-your-selfer's hands. Those plans are constrained by what we can call "common denominators": acceptable (already in the domain), adaptable (functional) styles at affordable prices. In some ways, they're like paint-by-number kits: follow the directions carefully and your product comes out like the picture on the cover. In good hands, those plans meet the usefulness criterion. In very good hands, they can even prove generative (*Better Homes and Gardens* features innovative variations on its own plans). In no set of hands can they be influential (remember, they're already in the domain).

CHAPTER 7

Constraints for Creativity in Advertising

What can we learn from Shirley Polykoff? What can we learn from Leo Burnett? What can we learn from Rosser Reeves?

What constraints structure the creativity problem in advertising? At least three—an overall *goal constraint* (selling), a constant *task constraint* (the product), and a specific *goal constraint* (the selling promise or strategy). In this chapter, I call them the Goal, the Product, and the Strategic Constraint. We'll look at each separately and then see how three creative greats combined the three—selling products via strategic promises.

THE GOAL CONSTRAINT

The primary *goal constraint* in advertising is functional. The function is to persuade you (and me) to buy a product, elect a person, visit a place.

Any ad that gets you to buy *X*, me to vote *Y*, or us to visit *Z* meets the minimum creativity criteria—usefulness. More creative is one that generates its own variants (called pool-outs in the business), one that becomes a continuing, convincing campaign. Most creative is the truly influential campaign that changes a domain, either the product domain or the domain of advertising itself.

THE PRODUCT CONSTRAINT

The creative heads of the agencies that (famously) introduced the Volkswagen (Bill Bernbach), the Marlboro man (Leo Burnett), or the Hathaway man (David Ogilvy) (Higgins, 1965; Millman, 1988), all stressed the importance of knowing the product. Knowing means knowing *everything* about it, how it works, whom it appeals to, why it appeals to them (what need it meets or can meet), what the competition is doing.

Knowing everything is critical if you're working on a "difficult" product, of which there are two kinds—a parity product or a radical product (Twichell, 2000, p. 118). Parity means equal (no product difference) and common (widely used). Most parity products are package goods, products that come in packages, sit on shelves, and are not new. Just imagine an aisle in your supermarket or drugstore.

A parity product is difficult because an ad has to add value to it. Rosser Reeves (1961) demonstrated the problem this way. Holding two coins, and pointing to one, he said, "My job is to make you think that *this* quarter is more valuable than (pointing to the other) *that* one" (p. 11). Substitute white bread or shampoo or pain reliever for quarter. See the challenge?

Radical products have a different problem. They're not just new, they break social taboos. The difficulty is different; an ad has to change the product's domain by making it acceptable. Shirley Polykoff did this for Clairol hair color in 1955. In that year, in her words, "Hair coloring had about the same social acceptance as cigarettes and lipsticks before the First World War" (Polykoff, 1975, p. 26). Substitute tattoo or body piercing for hair color. See the challenge?

THE STRATEGIC CONSTRAINT

Strategies are practiced, successful-in-the-past ways of approaching problems. In the problem–solving literature, they take the form of "if . . . then" rules: *if* this situation, *then* this action. Different advertising agencies work with, and are known for, different strategies. Famous "creatives" (writers and art directors) are famous for strategies that solved parity and radical product problems. Three of the most famous are Shirley Polykoff, Leo Burnett, and Rosser Reeves.

Shirley Polykoff: "If the Customer Were Me . . ."

BC (Before Clairol), hair coloring had definite drawbacks. The product itself was one problem. Who used it was the other.

BC colorings coated your hair, came off on your clothes, and were truly transient. Clairol was a genuinely new product. Instead of coating the outside, Clairol penetrated the keratin outer layer of your hair, leaving the color inside, on the shaft, where it couldn't come off. The color was so permanent that (perfect for repeat sales) without regular use, your roots would give you away.

Solving the product problem was necessary, but not sufficient to satisfy the *goal constraint*, persuading "respectable" women (your mother or grandmother) that hair coloring was permissible. In 1955, only "fast" women (jet–setters, models, actresses, and other "professional" beauties) dyed, did, touched up, or changed their hair color. Painting your hair, like painting your face, was a social taboo . . . *unless nobody knew.* That became the campaign strategy (Polykoff, 1975).

"Does she . . . or doesn't she?" asked Shirley.

The *she* pictured in the Miss Clairol campaign was the model of respectability, in Shirley's words, a "shirtwaist type." Since this was advertising, *she* also had to be "the proverbial girl on the block who's a little prettier than your wife"; in other words, "the average model with her face washed" (p. 29). The real clincher was adding a child whose hair color and condition (soft and shiny) were very close to hers.

Persuading the American woman that hair coloring was no longer risque led to the introduction of different Clairol products designed to solve different coloring problems.

Lady Clairol was better—faster, gentler, more subtle—at blonding.

"Is it true that blondes have more fun?" asked Shirley.

Loving Care's color was sheer enough to not show on hair that still had its own color. It only showed on the stray grays that had lost theirs.

"Hate that gray?" asked Shirley. *"Wash it away."*

I've already suggested the *strategy* behind this series of successes, "If the customer were me . . . ." While Shirley never said that directly, she certainly suggested it. Asked about the breakthrough Miss Clairol campaign, her reply was: "I guess my whole life wrote that campaign" (p. 20).

Shirley knew her customer better than anybody, in fact, intimately, because she was Clairol's ideal customer, the blond girl whose hair darkened at age 15, who made regular visits to Mr. Nicolas's beauty parlor, where *her* hairdresser kept her much admired "naturally" blond hair blond—and her blonding secret (p. 21).

Every woman—not just a born blond—was "naturally" some shade lighter, some years earlier. Many years after Polykoff made hair color respectable and Clairol successful here, J. Walter Thompson used the same sort of permissive mother-child pairings to introduce Helene Curtis hair color in Japan. The campaign was initiated by the women in Thompson's Tokyo office, who brought in pictures of themselves as children to prove that they once were "natural" brunettes.

Leo Burnett: "If the Product Had a Personality . . ."

There's an old game in which you think up analogies. You take an object (a person or place) and say, "If X were a color, a feeling, a tree, a piece of music, etc., she'd be a . . .?" In advertising, the object is your product; your best analogy, the product's personality. In the best advertising (of this kind), the personality personifies the product's promise. In the worst, the personality overwhelms the product.

David Ogilvy came close, but no one ever beat Leo Burnett at this game. "Lurking in every product that deserves success," he said, "is a reason for being and a reason for buying. . . . The trick is to make it interesting and exciting" (Lorin, 2001, p. 62). I like this quote because it includes our three advertising *constraints*. One stems from the *product*. Not every product deserves success; a good ad can only sell a bad product once. Another points to the *goal*, selling. The third gets down to the business of advertising, the *strategy*, the trick. Burnett's trick was giving a product a *selling personality*.

What promise does the Green Giant personify? Produce from a land of plenty. Niblets (the original brand name) of corn so sweet they squirt if you stick your fingernail in a kernel. Plump peas from pods as green as the Giant himself. The Giant himself looks like a character from Greek or Roman myth, a masculine Ceres, the goddess of agriculture from whose name came "cereal." He could also be a fairytale character, a friendly, jollier version of the giant who grew that very big beanstalk that Jack climbed. His personality promises that his produce—which comes in a package and sits on a shelf (in or out of a freezer), the ultimate parity product—is sweeter, fresher, better.

What promise does the Marlboro man personify? The Giant's personality added value to the product. The Marlboro Man's added it to the user. Cigarettes and beers are really cosmetics. When brewers say that young people "drink with their eyes," they mean that drinks (parity products) sell for what they convey about the drinker, not about the brew (Kanner, 1999, p. 124). The same is true of cigarettes. Before 1955, the Marlboro brand said nothing male smokers (the big target) wanted said about themselves. In Burnett's words, it was "a sissy smoke . . . a tea room smoke" (Twichell, 2000, p. 129). It not only had a sissy filter, but a bright red one. Why red? To conceal lipstick stains (Twichell, p. 130).

Burnett re-branded that sissy smoke using the *ur*-symbol of masculinity, the cowhand riding and roping in mythical Marlboro Country, often alone on the range, sometimes herding or sitting around a campfire with others of his ilk. Even without the Man's wrist tattoo, flipping open a new box (tough, solid, "branded" with a bright red V) of Marlboros announced that the smoker too was one of his ilk. The smokers weren't just men. I remember a hit song with one repetitive line "I wanna be a cowgirl. . . ." Leo Burnett knew. Everyone wanted to be the Marlboro Man. Almost 50 years later, they still do. The Giant is mythical, ditto the Marlboro Man. In the advertising business, so is their maker.

Rosser Reeves: "If the Product Made *One* Promise . . ."

Leo Burnett added value to parity products by giving them unique personalities. Rosser Reeves did it by pre-empting the single most important benefit a product could deliver. Pre-empt means seizing before anyone else can. Pre-emptive claims work because of the way memory works.

Remember those associative networks from chapter 3? If we draw one for white bread and Wonder Bread (see Figure 7.1), it's easy to see how pre-emptive claims work. Once customers learned that "Wonder builds strong bodies 12 ways," any other nutritional claim only served to remind them of Wonder.

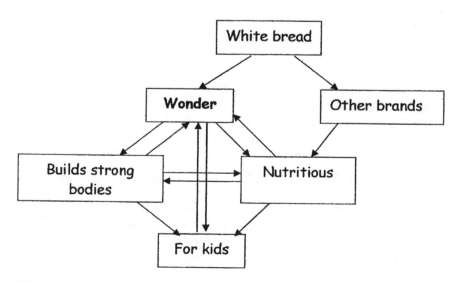

FIGURE 7.1. Wonder Bread network.

The pre-emptive claim is a *strategic constraint*. Reeves gave the claim a name: the *U.S.P.* or Unique Selling Proposition. Why the singular—proposition, not propositions? "The consumer tends to remember just one thing from an advertisement—one strong claim, or one concept" (Reeves, 1961, p. 34). Since the product has to deliver on the claim, there's a strong *product constraint* here as well.

The U.S.P. was the *strategic constraint* behind claims/campaigns for package goods like candy made with "milk chocolate that melts in your mouth, not in your hand" (M&Ms), the detergent that "softens hands while you do dishes" (Palmolive), a toothpaste so effective that "only a dentist can give your teeth a better flouride treatment" (Colgate), and analgesics that "act twice as fast to relieve pain" (Bufferin), or work "like a doctor's prescription" (Anacin). The claims themselves were supported by demos, showing how each product provided its benefit.

The most (in)famous commercial associated with Reeves demonstrated both how the problem felt (the tension headache) and how the solution (Anacin) worked. It also demonstrates how much Reeves knew about *cognitive constraints*. If you (can) recall, our heads hold between three and seven items in short-term memory. Everything in the Anacin spot was done in threes. There were three boxes in the silhouetted head of the sufferer; a hammer repeatedly and loudly banged an anvil in the central one. There were three dishes with the three pain killers that do three things (relieve pain, relax tension, soothe irritability). The tag line reached its crescendo by repeating itself three times (For fast, Fast, FAST relief). The commercial and its pool-outs (slightly different versions) ran repeatedly for more than three years.

There's a second meaning to U.S.P., Unique Selling Personality. Think about Madge the Manicurist, softening her customer's cuticles in Palmolive liquid detergent, or about O. J. (before Nicole) juking through airports for Hertz. Madge was an authority on soft hands, O. J. an authority on speed. Hard claims don't always need hammer-hard sells.

What Can We Learn From Polykoff, Burnett, and Reeves?

Everything we *can't* learn from current advertising. There were far fewer commercials when Shirley, Leo, and Rosser were running agencies. Today, the clutter is ubiquitous. There are too many commercials, too many interchangeable products, too many interchangeable ads. Why? Because too many advertisers and agencies are working with *too few constraints*.

TOO MUCH CLUTTER, TOO FEW CONSTRAINTS

Too Many Commercials

I watched commercials one night. In a single break, there were eight: one for hair coloring, two for food (fast, snack), two for sales (appliances, cars), and three for shows (two TV programs, one movie). I only remembered because I wrote them down. Unfortunately, no one at the agency or client remembers, or knows (like Rosser Reeves did), the *cognitive constraints* on how many separate pieces of information our brains can process.

Too Many Interchangeable Products

To see just how many there are in the hair-color category, I went to my computer and a local drugstore. There are still only two major hair-color brands, Clairol and L'Oreal, each with multiple (self-competing) entries. On the Clairol home page, I found eight permanent colors (including the original Miss Clairol), four semi-permanent ones (lasting between six and twenty-four shampoos), thirteen lighteners (highlights, etc.), and two color lines for men. While L'Oreal's page only featured five, in the same semi-, permanent, and lightening categories, I found more in the drugstore.

Since I was in the drugstore, I walked to the headache remedy aisle and took a count. Anacin (still promising fast relief) was still there, along with its early competitors, Bayer and Bufferin. There were several sorts of Excedrin (p.m., extra strength, aspirin–free, migraine) and Tylenol (arthritis strength, regular, and extra strength), plus Motrin (migraine headache), Advil, Benedryl (sinus headache), and the generic brands that duplicate each. When you have a headache, do you know what kind of headache you have? You'd better.

What *constraints* are violated here? *Cognitive.* Not only are there too many choices, but to choose you have to know what kind of headache you have. *Goal.* Why buy a brand name when a no-name generic has the same active ingredients and is cheaper? (Now you know why there are so many coupons.)

Too Many Interchangeable Ads

In *Reality in Advertising* (1961), Rosser Reeves wrote that fewer than 20 percent of the ads in magazines had a U.S.P. Is it still true? To find out, I took Reeves' suggestion: "Pick up a magazine and leaf through it" (p. 50).

One magazine I picked up was *Better Homes and Gardens*. The back cover depicted "the usual stunning picture" (p. 51), in this case, a sort-of-silver-colored Toyota splashing up spray on a wet surface with the words "I am Corolla. Hear me roar!" under the front grill. Inside the front cover was a double-page spread: One side showed a sort-of-silver-colored Chevy and the words "Just like you, we'll be there" above the hood; the other side showed a dad's hand on a child's head in the foreground. Both ads had their own "little deluge" (p. 51) of expected automotive promises: "dependability, value, fun" (Toyota); "dependable, protection, the right stuff" (Chevy).

"Where is the proposition? Where the uniqueness?" (p. 50) I said, echoing Reeves.

What about food? Without naming names, there was a bottled drink in "five fruity flavors [with] just five calories"; a cereal promising "100% good taste"; a macaroni and cheese dinner "closer to home"; brownies ready "in just 5 minutes"; a shortcake making a "big impression"; a pilaf as "a recipe for change"; a dad taking his baby's pacifier to eat onion dip with; hot dogs that got "plump" when cooked; cheese as "an excellent source of calcium." None of these is a U.S.P. At best, the photography might make you hungry for (generic) macaroni and cheese, hot dogs, or brownies.

What about cosmetics? I picked up *Vogue*. There were lots of ads for lots of creams with lots of interchangeable claims ("youthful-looking skin," "reverses the effects of time," "fights signs of aging," "firming," "anti-aging"). Ditto with ads for lipsticks and eye-shadows ("rich color, intense moisture," "more color, more intensity"). There was one U.S.P.—"Wet to set in 1 minute flat."

What's the product category? Anyone who's ever waited for nail polish to dry (without messing it up) knows. What's the product? Maybelline Express Finish. This is a smart company with a good agency. Even the name states the claim.

Too Much Entertaining, Too Little Selling

Only a market leader can afford to entertain you. Kodak can sell taking pictures ("Share moments. Share life"). Bud can sell comradarie ("Whassssupppppp?"). Nike can just say "Just do it" (like Michael Jordan, et cetera).

Littler guys can't afford to entertain you. Did you watch the Super Bowl with all the dot.com commercials? Did you know what they were for? A lot of us didn't. And a lot of them (the dot.coms) aren't in business anymore.

Some bigger guys can't afford to entertain you either. The classic example is Alka-Seltzer's series of silly overeaters ("I can't believe I ate the whole thing," "Try it—you'll like it," "That's a-some a-spicy meatballs!") which were laughed at, remembered, and rewarded with advertising awards. The problem was they didn't sell Alka-Seltzer. An upset stomach isn't funny when it's your stomach that's upset.

If you remember the punchline, but not the product, there's no *product constraint* driving the commercial. Without a product constraint, there's no *goal constraint* (selling the product), either.

TWO CONVERSATIONS: COMMERCIAL ART

So far, this chapter has been mostly about words, but advertising is about words and pictures—or to use agency vocabulary, about copy and layout. To remedy the imbalance, we consider constraints from the viewpoint of the art director.

Ideas Versus Visuals

Seymour Leichman (personal interview, January 20, 2002), an art director who also teaches at Pratt, thinks of constraints as rules to be learned. The basic one he calls "controlling the space." The first thing an art director draws when he sits down to design an ad is a box. "We live in that box," he tells his students. The box is the size of the print ad or the length of the television commercial.

What goes in the box?

There's always type. Leichman teaches his students to use type, to choose a type face, as a design element that "invites the reader in." One assignment he gives is taking something a student loves (a poem, the start of a favorite story) and setting it so that someone else will want to read it. The two constraints given in his instructions—"Make it seductive and make it legible"—are exemplified in the classic Volkswagen print campaign. The biggest element was a single word, LEMON.

Sometimes, not often enough, you find an idea in the box. Ideas illustrate, demonstrate what your product promises. Coming up with a look (the big LEMON and the little CAR) or a demo (below) that your product can *own* involves, Leichman says, learning the difference between "an idea and a visual."

An idea is the graphic equivalent of a *strategic constraint*. A good one, like a good strategy, leads to multiple executions. For an underarm deodorant, a great idea was "Raise Your Arm if You're Sure." (You don't even have to see the ads to know what they look like, or what they promise.) In contrast, a visual might picture a group or an individual dressed in starched, pristine, white linen. Any deodorant could use the visual. Sure owned the idea.

"Raise Your Arm if You're Sure" is what Leichman calls the "whole package," indivisible copy and art, a *graphic promise*.

Campaign Ideas

Ivan Sherman (personal correspondence, February 26, 2002), the other art director I interviewed, has spent a career coming up with whole packages. His response to my initial question about constraints was, "If we tried to create without constraints, the ads would just be noise."

Two campaigns with "ideas," those combined *strategic-graphic constraints* that Seymour Leichman talked about, were created for Tums and Nicorette.

Just as Sure owned "Raise Your Arm," and Wonder Bread owned "builds strong bodies," Tums owns calcium. It does so because its advertising had two visual ideas. One involved demonstration, animation, a stomach on fire until a Tums tablet (*cum* calcium), dissolving into powder, put out the fire. The fire stands for the problem, heartburn; the powder stands for the solution, Tums' acid-diluting action. The other involved type, an almost unwrapped roll of Tums with the "UM" prominently left at one end and the letters "CALCI" behind it. Together the letters spelled out the promise: calcium.

The Tums campaign wasn't done at Ted Bates, but it certainly embodies Rosser Reeves' approach to advertising: "If the product made one promise . . ."

The Nicorette campaign used Shirley Polykoff's approach, "If the consumer were me . . ." The client and the agency both wanted a smoker on the account (Ivan Sherman was the smoker). Why? To find the "emotional links" that would grab the consumer. Links that only smokers would know about, links like making the smoker feel like a "hero" (versus feeling that he can't give it up), giving the smoker credit (he made up his mind to quit), avoiding lectures (no dirty ashtrays, no smoke).

In addition to the emotional links, there was the graphic promise. A Nicorette pack (the solution) breaking through a link chain (the problem). A whole package.

WHAT HAVE WE LEARNED?

Do constraints structure the creativity problem in advertising? Certainly for the Shirleys and Leos and Rossers who devised them.

Which creativity criteria did their campaigns meet? All sold their product (check off usefulness). All pooled out beautifully (check off generativity) and, I imagine, easily. James Webb Young (1975), whose thin book on producing ideas was given to every new copywriter at J. Walter Thompson when I began in the business (pre-PhD, I was a copywriter at Thompson, a creative group head at Bates), said it succinctly: "A good idea has, as it were, self-expanding qualities. It stimulates those who see it to add to it" (p. 53). Those who add to it are the writers and art directors—not necessarily the ones who originated the idea—who keep the campaign (and its progeny—convincing extensions, like Marlboro Lights and all those other Clairol colorings) going year after year.

Did any change a domain? Check "yes" for Shirley, who surely changed hair coloring. What about advertising? Rosser systematized on an agency-wide basis what earlier admen (his first chorus) like Gerard Lambert ("Listerine stops halitosis!") and Claude Hopkins ("Pepsodent gets rid of film on teeth!") did individually. Rosser raised the bar for the business. What about Leo? Burnett didn't invent the selling personality, but he perfected the form and, like Rosser, taught an agency how to do it.

In actuality, all three of our strategists taught an industry—serving as the *first chorus* for copywriters and art directors (like Sherman and Leichman) who continue to create *effective* advertising using the constraints that they codified.

CHAPTER 8

Constraints for Creativity in Music

What can we learn from Debussy? What can we learn from Stravinsky? What can we learn from Schoenberg? What can we learn from Copland? What can we learn from Ives? What can we learn from Berg?

What constraints structure the creativity problem in music? Specialized *task constraints* that turn sounds into music, which—as Leonard Bernstein (1976, p. 15) pointed out—can be thought of as heightened speech. Why? Because like speech, music consists of a limited set of elements (tones instead of words), organized into patterns (measures instead of sentences) by structural constraints on rhythm, melody, and harmony.

Since some, many, probably most of you, are not musicians, this chapter starts with a section (fundamental to musicians) to help you "hear" the differences between rhythm, melody, and harmony. Much of this material is modeled after Copland (1953).

STRUCTURAL TASK CONSTRAINTS: RHYTHM, MELODY, HARMONY

Rhythm is the most basic constraint. With two legs, you walk in a two-step: the rhythm goes one-two, one-two, one-two. If you march, the first step is accented: <u>one</u>-two, <u>one</u>-two, <u>one</u>-two. If you waltz, the rhythm changes from <u>one</u>-two, <u>one</u>-two to <u>one</u>-two-three, <u>one</u>-two-three, <u>one</u>-two-three. Read the counts out loud to hear the difference in the rhythms. Music is traditionally written with the same number of beats or counts, to a measure. Measures are separated by vertical lines, which means our walking rhythm would look something like this:

/ <u>one</u>-two / <u>one</u>-two /

Since many simple tunes share this one-two rhythm, we can add a well-known tune—"Twinkle, Twinkle, Little Star"—to our rhythmic diagram. (If you sing the tune to yourself, you will hear why star and are each have a measure to themselves.)

/ <u>Twink</u>-le / <u>twink</u>-le / <u>lit</u>-tle / <u>star</u> /
/ <u>How</u>-I / <u>won</u>-der / <u>what</u>-you /<u>are</u> /

The tune is the melody, made up of notes or tones, taken in the case of *Twinkle* from the scale of C major. Traditional Western scales consist of seven tones or notes constrained by the size of the intervals between the notes. This is most easily seen on a piano keyboard.

Going from one white key to the next white key with a black key between (C to D in Figure 8.1) is called a whole step; going from a white to a white key with no black key between (E to F) is a half step. Scales are made up in the following order: two whole steps, one–half step, three whole steps, one half–step. Starting from the leftmost, or lower C, there are two whole steps (C-D, D-E), then a half–step (E-F), then three more whole steps (F-G, G-A, A-B) and a final half–step (A-C) to the rightmost or higher C.

The relationships between the notes of any scale are based on the physical properties of sounds, which are vibrations. When any sound source

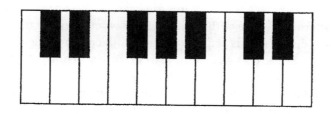

C   D   E   F   G   A   B   C   D   E

FIGURE 8.1. Piano keyboard. Letters are the names of the notes.

(voices, steps, instruments) vibrates, it produces not only its own tone, but also a series of overtones. The first overtone is an octave higher than the base tone. In the C major scale, the base tone (or tonic) is the lower or left-most C, the first overtone is the higher or rightmost C. The second over-tone (or dominant) is G, the fifth note of the scale. Between them, C and G identify the tonality of a piece written in the scale of C major. If we write out the note names for the first eight measures of *Twinkle,* you'll see that the first phrase starts on C, and ends on G, while the second returns to C.

/ <u>Twink</u>-le / <u>twink</u>-le / <u>lit</u>-tle / <u>star</u> /
/ C-C / G-G / A-A / G/
/ <u>How</u>-I / <u>won</u>-der / <u>what</u>-you / <u>are</u> /
/ F-F / E-E / D-D / C/

When composers want to add surprise or suspense to a piece, they make temporary detours (or modulations) to more or less closely related keys. For example, Mozart began and ended his twelve variations on *"Twinkle"* in C. In between, he modulated many times to the key of G (the dominant), which differs from the key of C in having the note F raised a half-step. The raised F, called F sharp (F#), is the black key between F and G. The tension arising from a modulation is relaxed when the music returns (or resolves) to its base key. Multiple modulations and returns produce a sense of goal-directed movement in longer compositions.

Both rhythm and melody are organized horizontally; they move for-ward in time. Harmony, the third constraint, is organized vertically. Harmonies consist of chords—notes played at the same time. Notes are consonant when their vibration patterns coincide. By extension, chords are heard as consonant when they consist of notes from the same overtone series. For example, we can build a consonant C chord by playing C and G together. We can extend this chord by adding E, which is the next note in the overtone series: C-E-G. Chords are heard as dissonant when their vi-bration patterns interfere with each other, or when they are unfamiliar. As we shall see, dissonance is central to much 20th century music.

A crisis in music occurred at the start of the last century when the basic tonal constraints—the melodic and harmonic ones—became so distended that they could no longer structure and thus unify a composition (Morgan, 1991; Sessions, 1979). As in art and architecture, new *task constraints* were needed. The first part of this chapter will focus on the very different solution paths to this problem taken by three great innovators in 20th century com-position. As in art and architecture, the paths and the novel constraints de-rived from each composer's quite different first choruses and goal constraints.

The second part of the chapter will focus on thematic or *subject constraints*. The commonality among the composers considered will be their use of existing themes or motifs in the development of their music. A conversation with a contemporary composer concludes the chapter.

STYLISTIC CONSTRAINTS: STRUCTURING DISSONANCE

In the first half of the 20th century, the domain of music was radically expanded by three composers, each with the same *goal constraint:* increased expressive power, each with a focus on a different *task constraint:* Debussy on harmony, Stravinsky on rhythm, and Schoenberg on melody.

Interestingly, their goal was not only common among composers at the close of the 19th century, it was the *cause* of the breakdown in tonality. As the start of this chapter showed, the tonal system developed by Bach in the 16th century used related sounds—tonic and dominant notes and chords, for example—to produce music of great orderliness, structural clarity, and unity. The result was what we call Classical: logical, objective, impersonal, and the antithesis of the 19th century Romantic preference for the expressive, subjective, and sentimental. Sentimentality led to an emphasis on extra-musical meanings, like the Wagnerian leitmotif; expressivity to the exploitation of sounds for their own sake: striking, sharply contrasting, often isolated, details, dissonances that were no longer transitory modulations from a consonant home key, but sustained. Ambiguity was undermining both clarity and unity (Morgan, 1991).

All three of our composers' solutions to the expressivity versus ambiguity problem involved the actual heightening of dissonance.

Sensibilité: Debussy and Harmony

Sensibilité, is a French word suggesting delicacy of taste, extreme responsiveness to nuances, heightened feeling (Schonberg, 1970, p. 442). It describes Debussy's path, which turned the problem into its own solution. Instead of disambiguating tonality, Debussy embraced ambiguity (precluding unity) by emphasizing the exquisite, often exotic moment (precluding movement).

Like Monet, Debussy was labeled an Impressionist. Remember Monet's "envelope" that surrounds things? For Monet the envelope was light; for Debussy it was sound. His music, his envelope, is indeed quite similar to

Monet's—shimmering, shifting, mosaic, surface. The difference is that harmonies (rather than hues) engage the ear (rather than the eye) for an instant, then shift, merge, and disappear. Singular harmonies shift rather than flow, merge rather than move. *Nothing develops. Everything is.*

Mozart holds our ear with movement. "Twinkle Twinkle" is varied in thirteen different ways, each constrained by the tune which—elaborated, condensed, inverted, transposed—disappears and reappears and continually leads us forward.

To hold the ear without movement, Debussy's harmonies had to be sonorous, rich, and strange. Where did they come from? The answer is like a fairy tale's. Debussy's first choruses come from long ago, and from lands far away. His sources are unfamiliar sounds, scales with intervals that ring foreign in our ears. This of course means that he was precluding consonance.

Long ago meant early church music (Thompson, 1967). From longest ago were medieval modes or modal scales. One of these, the Dorian, has eight notes, like our familiar scales do, and begins on D. The critical difference is that a modern D major scale has two sharps (on the keyboard, C# and F# are the black notes to the right of the white C and F keys), but the Dorian scale has no sharps. A "modern" chord constructed with the first, third, and fifth notes in the D major scale would be D-F#-A. It would sound both familiar and consonant to our ears. The corresponding "modal" chord would be D-F-A. Its sound would be surprising and dissonant, exactly what Debussy sought: surprise and dissonance serve to heighten feeling, *sensibilité*.

The other two church modes were the eighth-note Phrygian and the pentatonic scale, which constrained the number of tones to five. The chords in "La Cathedrale Engloutie" (1910) ("The Sunken Cathedral") shift between these modes rather than modulating between related keys. The "Cathedrale" also echoes another early and churchly chorus, the melodic counterpoint of Gregorian chant.

In addition to these borrowing, Debussy devised his own whole-tone scale. Like the church modes, it has unfamiliar intervals (six equal whole steps) and produces dissonant-sounding chords. "L'apres midi d'un faune" (1894) closes with the whole-tone scale. It starts with an undulating flute solo derived from more recent (16th century) liturgical music, Palestrina's "melodic arabesques which create their effect through contour and through their interweaving" (Fish, 1997, p. 200). The quote is Debussy's.

Far away meant the mysterious Orient. To a Western ear, the strangeness of Far Eastern music—Japanese, Javanese—comes as much from its seeming stillness as from its exotic tones. The tones derive from different scales, including the pentatonic. The stillness follows the independence of its chord structures. The focus, like that of yoga, is on the now, the present sound, not its development or movement from the sound preceding or to the sound following. The gongs, bells, clappers, and rattles of the Javanese gamelang orchestra (heard at the Exposition Universelle of 1889–90) produced pulsations that contained, Debussy wrote, ". . . every nuance, even the ones we no longer have names for. The tonic and the dominant had become empty shadows of use only to stupid children" (p. 203). (Nuance, *sensibilité*.)

A gong, bell, or rattle sounds, reverberates, dissipates. "Pagodes" sounds like one extended pentatonic chord that finally fades (Nicols, 1972).

Of course, there were first choruses from not so long ago or so far away. One of the most important was Chopin's pedaling technique, which Debussy called "the art of turning the pedal into a kind of *breathing*" (Thompson, 1967, p. 251). Debussy's own pedaling aimed to blend his harmonies into a "sonorous halo" (Thompson, p. 251). In "La Cathedrale Engloutie," a continuous pedal merges the moving chord blocks into sounds suggestive of waves or bells tolling beneath the sea. The blocks are identically structured, moving in parallel up and down the keyboard to create a single, static harmony. (Nothing develops. Everything is.)

The choruses, initially disparate and unrelated to each other, combine in the defining characteristics of Debussy's radical harmonic constraints. Surface, nuance, *sensibilité* are the major constraints, the new goal criteria. They are reached by a *series of related constraints* on the prevalent tonal system: one precludes unity (The chords are independent, unrelated), a second precludes movement (The chords shift rather than modulate), the third precludes consonance (Since they are based on multiple modes and scales, their dissonances cannot be resolved).

A fourth constraint emerged from these three. It precluded traditional musical structures to promote novel scaffoldings. The traditional, easily identified, forms of Western music (e.g., variation, fugue, sonata) depend for their internal development on a tonal center. Pieces with less specific formal structures were called preludes. Each of Debussy's 24 preludes has a different form. We've already talked about the parallel chord progressions that structure one of them, "La Cathedrale." In "Des Pas sur la Neige" (1910) ("Foorsteps in the Snow"), a four-note motif in the left hand repetitively moves up and down a step, while the right hand plays a fragmentary and never–repeated melody. "Voiles" is built entirely from the whole-tone scale. (See Table 8.1).

TABLE 8.1. Debussy's Constraints

Goal	Sub-goals	Task constraints
Sensibilité		
	1. *The ambiguous*	Preclude *unity*
		→ Promote *independent, unrelated chords*
	2. *The moment*	Preclude *movement*
		→ Promote *shifting harmonies*
	3. *The exotic*	Preclude *consonance*
		→ Promote *multiple, unfamiliar tonalities*

What Can We Learn From Debussy?

Something we've already learned from Monet. How an ambiguous (and ambitious) *goal constraint* necessitates a novel series of *task constraints* that, over time, clarify and realize the goal. Monet's goal was to show how light, at this moment, breaks up. Debussy's goal substituted sound for light: sounds (chords instead of colors) break up (shifting one to another instead of modulating one into another) moment to moment.

Another lesson is that, as sound and form become freer for the composer, they become more and more difficult for the listener. With Debussy, the difficulty lies in ever increasing and unfamiliar dissonances. Unfamiliar things make us uncomfortable. We don't like feeling uncomfortable, and therefore don't like the source of our discomfort. But dislike and discomfort should be separated in making judgments. We can only really know if we like or dislike something when we have become familiar, and therefore comfortable, with it.

Primitivism: Stravinsky and Rhythm

Stravinsky's answer to the expressivity versus ambiguity problem involved not harmonic, but rhythmic dissonance. Debussy's harmonic dissonances precluded movement (Nothing happens). Paradoxically, Stravinsky's rhythmic ones restored momentum by precluding time, musical time that is, measured in beats like the rhythms we "heard" at the start of this chapter.

Stravinsky's strategy was to eliminate predictability (Oliver, 1995). This meant precluding the constant number of beats in each measure (between each pair of vertical lines) that made the rhythm metronomic, regular: / one-two / one-two / one-two / etc. To promote unpredictability, Stravinsky substituted a base set of shorter and longer rhythms to be combined and recombined in differing sized groups, with displaced accents, and in irregular asymmetric orders like / one-two / one-two / one-two-three / one-two-three-four-five /. *Nothing is predictable. Everything happens.*

Where did Stravinsky's radical rhythmic solution to the ambiguity problem come from? "First" first choruses; the Russian sounds and Russian rhythms of the composer's childhood. The adjectives Stravinsky used to describe the sounds of St. Petersburg suggest his own sounds: a *bristling* fife-and-drum band, the *rail-scraping* noise of the horse-drawn streetcars, the trilling *wires* of a balalaika orchestra. The accordion (a percussive instrument) that he recalled with nostalgia haunts "Petroushka." Other remembered sounds were abrupt, sharp, and piercing: the shrill cries of the street vendors, the shriller cry of the new telephones, the boom of the noon gun at the Peter and Paul Fortress (Stravinsky & Croft, 1962, pp. 24–32).

The sources of his rhythmic memories—syncopated, repetitive, percussive, primal—were the Russian peasantry (dances like the *kazochok* or *presiatka* are part of "Petroushka"; unharmonized tunes with short, repetitive, two or three note motifs form the fragmented mosaic of "Le Sacre") and the Russian Church (the tolling bells of the Nikolovsky Cathedral and the obsessive chant of the Orthodox liturgy re-sound and resound in "Les Noces," and also later, in Latin, in the "Symphony of Psalms").

Stravinsky's childhood made him a true musical nationalist whose music evokes, without direct quotation, the sounds and rhythms of his homeland. He was not the first. There were also Glinka, Mussorgsky, and Rimsky-Korsokov, his composition teacher. Mussorgsky, like Glinka, utilized the irregularities of Russian folk music: irregularities of scale and rhythm, asymmetries in pattern. Rimsky's operas evoked the exoticism, the dazzling opulence of the Russian East that made "The Firebird" a dazzling success, and the Slavic pantheism that beat at the heart of "Le Sacre."

Debussy too was part of the first chorus. Stravinsky himself said that "'Le Sacre' owes more to Debussy than to anyone except myself" (Schonberg, 1970, p. 470). Its opening bassoon solo echoes the flute solo at the start of "L'apres midi d'un faune." The harmonic dissonances also follow Debussy. Chords appear solely for their colors, but the colors are more Stravinsky's, more barbaric than beautiful. Debussy's pedaling had liberated the piano from the percussion section; Stravinsky turned the entire orchestra into an insistent, pounding, percussive instrument.

Also unlike Debussy's, the chords were related to each other. Unlike anyone else's, they were related in a totally new way. In Stravinsky's restructuring, the primary relations are rhythmic rather than harmonic. "Le Sacre" is a ritual—a highly patterned act, repeated and repetitive, pagan and propulsive, sacred and sacrificial. Its pattern is constructed from melodic and rhythmic fragments that permute in transitory contractions and expansions. The fragments are sharply accented, relentlessly repeated, unpredictably shifted. (*Everything happens.*)

"Les Noces" is also a ritual, a rite of passage, a marriage. More abstract, stylized and austere than "Le Sacre," it too has a sacrificial virgin, a bride. It too is propelled by the coupling and uncoupling of rhythmic/melodic fragments, fragments that are played, sung, and accompanied by dance. There are four ceremonial tableaux: the hair of the bride is bound, the groom asks a parental blessing, the mothers lament, the couple is led to the bridal chamber. The orchestra is entirely percussive: four pianos, xylophones, bass drum, cymbals, cimbalon. Bells toll. The female solo—high-pitched, piercing, oriental—is a kind of sung speech. Piano and tympani count out the syllables.

The Russian-ness and ritualism of Stavinsky's revolutionary period resurface many times, particularly in the much later and liturgical "Symphony of Psalms." The high-pitched female voices are not as shrill as in "Les Noces," nor are the syllables as sharply accented in accompaniment. This is ritual once removed, distanced. Yet at the close, the pace is processional. Male and female choruses toll the chant. Candles flicker. The "Symphony," in Paul Rosenfeld's evocative prose, calls ". . . to mind the mosaic-gilded interior of the Byzantine domes that represent [the] Eastern world idea; one of those domes from whose vaulting the Christ and his Mother gaze piteously upon the accursed human race" (Leibowitz, 1969, p. 179). Piteously, once removed.

In essence, Stravinsky's achievement was to *constrain time* in two ways. One was *structural,* the other *experiential.* The blood races. The primal, the archaic, is present. (*Nothing is predictable. Everything happens*).

What Can We Learn From Stravinsky?

The interactive effects of the problem at hand and the first choruses that provide the elements for its solution. The problem (as we've already learned) was ambiguity. The first choruses were Russian and rhythmic, peasant dance, church chant, and earlier experiments by Russian composers in combining rhythms.

Tchaikovsky, for example, combined two rhythms in one measure to produce longer phrases with multiple accents. Putting / <u>one</u>-two / and / <u>one</u>-two-three / together, Tschaikovsky would have gotten / <u>one</u>-two-<u>three</u>-four-five / <u>one</u>-two-<u>three</u>-four-five / etc. More counts, more accents, but still regular, still predictable, still not Stravinsky—but a fine first chorus on which to improvise the irregular and the unpredictable.

Predictability: Schoenberg and Melody

The Schoenbergian solution to the ambiguity-tonality dilemma was the most radical. Debussy had precluded movement; Stravinsky, time. Schoenberg precluded the tonal system itself.

Bach had established a "well," but not perfectly, tempered system. Well-tempered meant that no tone or key (think note on the piano) was perfectly tuned, which made it possible for any key to modulate or move into any other key. Within this new constraint, Bach wrote "The Well-Tempered Clavier." Its 48 preludes and fugues, two in each of the major and minor keys, demonstrate (again Harold Schonberg's words) "Bach's kind of rightness, of inevitability, of intelligence, of logically organized sequences of notes" (Schonberg, 1970, p. 29).

All had been jettisoned in pursuit of expressivity. Schoenberg jettisoned the tonal system in order to restore the inevitability, the intelligence, the logic, the rightness. Precluding Bach's major and minor scales—each centered on a single, *most* important note—Schoenberg promoted a system organized around a series of twelve *equally* important notes. Nonetheless, his continuing and most critical first chorus was Bach.

The name "12-tone system" derives from the use of all 12 notes in an octave. If you go back to the keyboard diagram on page 103, and count the white and black notes between the leftmost and the rightmost C, the sum is 12. These notes are the basis of the "tone-row" which can be arranged in any order so long as all 12 are included. If the arrangement followed the way the notes appear on our keyboard, the tone-row would be: C, C# (black), D, D# (black), E, F, F# (black), G, G# (black), A, A# (black), and B. The major *task constraint* is this: the sequence is invariant. All notes must appear in row order, none can be repeated until all the others have sounded (Morgan, 1991). *Everything is predictable.*

Since a note can appear by itself, or successive notes can be combined to form a chord, harmony can be thought of as a sort of vertical melody, another way to traverse the row. Melody, harmony, and consonance are all precluded. For example, using our keyboard-order row, C alone could be played first, then C#, then the chord D, D#, and E. This chord consists of adjacent notes that are very distant, very unfamiliar overtones of each other. It would sound extremely dissonant to an unaccustomed ear.

Not that dissonant chords were novel. Much of Debussy's exoticism was based on dissonant chords. What was new in Schoenberg was their relationship to each other. Rather than being ambiguous and in need of resolution to a consonant home-key chord, they were unambiguously, *logically,* generated from the ordering of the whole row. Perhaps the *rightness* of his row would meet his *goal constraint*—to make dissonance as comprehensible as consonance (Strein, 1975).

Unfortunately for the goal, comprehension was (and still is) confounded by a number of things. To start, the 12-tone system is contextural, defined solely by the current context, the particular row. Since the row is based on arbitrary relationships, it must be learned.

What makes the learning difficult is the absence of repetition. Each composition is based on a completely different row. You can see the differences between—and the difficulty in following—two real rows used by Schoenberg. For the *Wind Quartet,* the row is E♭ (black), G, A, B, C# (black), C, B♭, D, E , F# (black), A♭, F. In the *String Quartet No. 4,* the row is D, C# (black), A, B♭ (black), F, E♭ (black), E, C, A♭ (black), G, F# (black), B.

To make things more difficult, in each composition, the row continuously varies.

The variation techniques went, not surprisingly, back to Bach. This is because the music, like much of Bach, is polyphonic, made of many voices. Each voice has its own melodic line, which serves as a counterpoint to the others. The simplest sort of polyphonic variation is imitation. In a round like "Row, Row, Row Your Boat," the voices all sing the same tune, but enter at different times. The second voice begins when the first reaches *"your"*; the third when the second gets to *"your"* again. The interest is in the interaction:

1st voice: Row, row, row your boat, gently down . . .

2nd voice: Row, row, row your boat, gently down . . .

3rd voice: Row, row, row your boat, gently . . .

Simple, not at all like Schoenberg. The more complicated polyphonic techniques he used are too complicated for this book: turning a row upside down (inversion), reading it backwards (retrogression or crab motion), or doing both simultaneously (retrograde inversion). They are also too complicated to hear. (Even Stravinsky needed extended exposure and explication.) When the ear cannot follow the peregrinations of an utterly orderly row, there is no movement. Without movement, nothing develops. *Everything is predictable. Nothing develops.*

What Can We Learn From Schoenberg?

The difficulty, mentioned many times already, of the new. The even greater difficulty of newness that is inaccessible without expert knowledge. Debussy discomforted, but he also seduced. The beauty of his chords elicited the extended listening that, over time, made his novelties comprehensible. Schoenberg leaves (nonmusically trained) listeners disoriented and, critically, disinclined to remedy their incomprehension.

SUBJECT CONSTRAINTS: I THINK I'VE HEARD THAT SONG BEFORE

Quotations, direct and other, are not new in music. What else are first choruses for? Mozart didn't write the "Twinkle" theme. It came from a French folk tune called "Avez direi-je mamam?" The theme itself constrains its transformations. Mozart first quotes it directly (here we can all hum along), then uses its outline as an armature on which the variations rest (humming along is harder, but still possible).

Notice that Mozart, a German, borrowed a French tune. Between Mozart and Mussorgsky, quotation became both more recondite and more provincial. Nonmusicians would not necessarily recognize the themes by Paganini on which Liszt and Brahms and Rachmaninoff based their respective variations. Quotation became indirect, outlines were absorbed, obscured in the variations, recondite. In the late 19th century in Europe, and the early 20th in America, a nonmusical event—nationalism—brought back borrowings from the vernacular, the national vernacular, the songs and dances, tunes and rhythms of a particular people, in short, provincial (Morgan, 1991).

A continuum of transformations turned folk quotation into modern music. Which part of the continuum you compose at (what and how you quote) depends, of course, on what's in your musical memory. Europeans (with long, homogeneous memories) began at the direct quotation end of the continuum and soon moved to the other, with compositions evocative, rather than imitative, of the ethos.

The simplest transformations presented the quoted theme itself with simple ("Twenty Hungarian Tunes," half by Bartok and half by Kodaly) or more elaborate (Bartok's "Fifty Hungarian Peasant Songs") accompaniment. One step further were new tunes to traditional dance rhythms (Russian in "Petroushka," Bohemian in the "Slavonic Rhapsodies"). Most complicated were the completely new compositions (Bartok's "Allegro Barbaro," Stravinsky's "Les Noces"). Their impact lay less in the novelty of their themes than in the exoticism of their tuning, tonality, and meter. We've already encountered these. Recall that the richness and strangeness in Debussy's chords came from medieval modes. One was the pentatonic, a fifth-note scale with foreign-sounding seventh chords, that pervades Bartok's first chorus, Hungarian folk song. Remember, too, the rhythmic innovations of Stravinsky, based on the brief, repetitive motifs and unequal meters characteristic of Russian folk music.

Americans (always more direct, born in a melting pot with multiple or simply shorter musical memories) tended to cluster at the direct quotation end of the continuum. Ives inserted "America" in "Flanders Field," Copland appropriated cowboy laments for "Billy the Kid" (Rich, 1995).

Much of Ives (dissonant, polytonal) is difficult, so having an American musical memory helps. Like Schoenberg's, Ives's music was polyphonic, many-voiced (a *task constraint*). "Columbia, the Gem of the Ocean," "De Camptown Races," and barn–fiddling with its jigs and reels—each in a different key—conclude the "Second Symphony." The difference is that the voices sound familiar; they move the music through the structural difficulties.

The sounds of childhood echo in Ives, as they did in Stravinsky. The difference here is that Ives (in "Three Places in New England," for example) recalls not only the individual sonorities (marching bands in Danbury) but recreates their raucous cacophonies (the bands marched past each other, their different tunes and conflicting tempos delightfully dissonant). "Three Places" is scored with the trumpets, trombones, and tubas of the marching band.

Ives called his "On the Pavements" a "take-off on street dancing." He didn't mean hip-hop. Street dancing in a small New England town was the beat of early morning, the "sounds of people going to and fro, all different steps, and sometimes all the same—the horses, fast trot, canter, sometimes slowing into a walk . . . an occasional trolley throwing all rhythm out (footsteps, horse and man)—then back again" (Morgan, 1991, p. 145). Current events and musical memory combine in notes for an unfinished piece. The tentative title was "Giants vs. Cubs, August, 1907, Polo Grounds." In the notes we find: "Johnny comes sliding home safe. Tune: 'Johnny Comes Marching Home'" (Schonberg, 1970, pp. 541–542). It's a Civil War song: Johnny comes marching home again. Hurrah! Hurrah!

Copland's incorporation of Americana was more conscious. The Latin American dances in "Danzo Cubano," "El Salon Mexico," or "Three Latin-American Sketches," the Shaker songs in "Appalachian Spring," the cowboy laments in "Rodeo" and "Billy the Kid" were not part of Copland's early musical memories. They were acquired via compilations and sheet music.

A quote regarding "El Salon" from the composer's autobiography explains his method:

> I began (as I often did) by collecting musical themes or tunes out of which a composition might eventually emerge. It seemed natural to use popular Mexican melodies for thematic material; after all, Chabrier and Debussy didn't hesitate to help themselves to the melodic richness of Spain. . . . My purpose was not merely to quote literally, but to heighten without in any way falsifying the natural simplicity of Mexican tunes (Copland & Perlis, 1984, p. 245).

Copland's south–of–our–border sounds ("El Mosco," "El Palo Verde," "La Jesusita") were borrowed from "Cancionero Mexicano," and "El Folk-Lore y la Musica Mexicana."

"Our Singing Country" and "Traditional Music of America" contributed folk and fiddle tunes for "Rodeo." The choreographer Agnes de Mille wrote out for Copland what she remembered of "I Ride an Old Paint." She also gave him specific requests. One—for a "Texas minuet"—was met with a syncopated arrangement of a waltz-like herding tune ("I Ride an Old Paint"). Lincoln Kirstein, the co-founder of the American Ballet Theater, gave him cowboy song books when he accepted the commission for "Billy." "Great Grand-Dad, Git Along Little Doggies, Goodbye, Old Paint, The Dying Cowboy" (which I remember, in part: "Oh bury me not on the lone prairie, where the coyote howls and the wind blows free"), directly and indirectly quoted, contribute to "Billy's" very American, very Western, prairie sound.

There is a last quotation, not at all folksy, that I like a lot because it ties an old familiar tune to the (still unfamiliar) 12-tone system of Schoenberg. The quotation is direct, Bach to Berg, tonal to atonal. "The Violin Concerto of 1935" is very moving in both the expressive and directional meanings of the word. What makes it moving (in both ways) is Bach's chorale and Berg's tone-row. The concerto is a memorial to Mahler's daughter, who died at age 18. The chorale begins and ends with the words *Es ist genug* (It is enough). The row—G, Bb, D, F#, A, C, E, G#, B, Db, Eb, F—has strong tonal "overtones." The first nine notes pair up in major and minor thirds. The last four combine (remember, a row can move horizontally or vertically) to form a favorite chord of Debussy's, the tritone. More critically, the last four notes of Berg's row are equivalent to the opening four notes of Bach's chorale (Morgan, 1991). A solo violin and four clarinets quote the chorale, directly, repeatedly, alternately. Bach's melody begins, merges, with Berg's. At the end is a completely tonal chord. A 12-tone work "resolves" into a totally tonal (B flat major) chord formed by the first four notes of Berg's utterly beautiful tone-row. Without the Bach, we couldn't hope to hum the Berg.

What Can We Learn From Copland, Ives, and Berg?

That instead of just being improvised on, first choruses can be inserted, integrated, into new works. Integrating the new with the already–known does two things. Both are related to our discussion of memory in chapter 3.

First, integration allows access to an established associative network, a scaffolding onto which we can append, and comprehend, the unknown. An old tune can make a new piece sound familiar. Ives is complex. "De Camptown Races" makes the "Second Symphony" accessible. Second, a fortuitous combination can lead us to re-examine, rather than simply recognize, the familiar. The Bach chorale, heard after its incorporation by Berg, has a bite, a 20th century edge. The well known, the quotation, sounds new.

Fortunately for those of us who have not acquired extensive associative networks of a musical sort, an important kind of Bach-Berg, old-new, connection underlies much contemporary composition. One contemporary composer who interposes or superimposes sounds, familiar and strange, in ways that make the one surprising and the other accessible, is Jonathan Kramer (personal interview, January 20, 2002).

A CONVERSATION: CONTRASTING CONSTRAINTS

Our conversation pointed out a number of contrasting constraints in Kramer's working methods and works. The first contrast was that between the *goal constraints* of conservatory and university training—continuity or coherence, exemplified by the multiple transformations of a base motif in a Mozart variation piece—and that of its graduates, surprise. Two contrasting ways of combining consistency and surprise are, first, being consistently unexpected or surprising, and second, being consistent in unexpected, surprising ways.

Consistent surprise could easily lead to formlessness; surprising consistencies—which I take as Kramer's goal constraint—to new forms. To accomplish this goal, he uses two contrasting approaches to composition, in which either the musical form or the musical materials are (initially) completely constrained. One of these compositional or *task constraints* is to start with form *sans* materials. Its contrast is starting with the materials *sans* form.

Starting without form involves what Kramer called his "fictional mode." The method mimics that of the novelist who first fully develops his characters before placing them in a situation where he can observe and record their interactions. Musically, it translates into selecting a set of materials—notes, chords, rhythmic figures, melodies, sonorities—and seeing how they interact. Their interactions determine the musical form. Starting without materials involves gestating the form—the musical gestures with their fleeting or stable moods and textures, rest and movement, degrees of predictability, tension and relaxation—prior to specifying the rhythms, melodies, and harmonies that will articulate the form.

Are there noticeable differences in the music generated by the two contrasting task constraints?

To find out, I listened first to a piece in which form preceded (and determined) materials. The form of "Renascence" (1974) involved presenting stasis and movement simultaneously. Stasis constricted scale, rhythm, and color; the scale to six notes; the meter to 2/4; the rhythm to simple quarter– and eighth–notes; the color to the sound of a single instrument, a clarinet, which is recorded and played back during the performance. The six notes ("close to traditional" Kramer called it) sounded strangely familiar—like the D major scale with its two sharps, F and C, but without its A.

Now, without the possibility of shifting tonality or rhythm, how would movement occur? It occurred in a surprisingly consistent way, by changes in density.

I listened several times to the piece. This is what I heard. "Renascence" starts with a single instrumental line. I became aware of a drone beneath the line, and then fragments of the line reappearing, creating a kind of counterpoint to the line. Several things began to increase—pitch differences, volume, dissonances, the frequency of a single motif, the number of layers of simultaneously played and replayed sounds, some like sirens. Gradually, the density and volume decreased. The piece dissipated on the drone alone.

A contrasting piece in which materials preceded form is "Surreality Check" (1989). Kramer called it his response to Surrealism, which presented familiar objects in strange ways, or shocking objects in banal ones. (Think of Magritte's cracked glass leaning against a blank wall under an emptied windowframe. The fragments retain the image seen through the glass prior to its breaking.)

"Surreality Check" presents well-known styles (e.g., Romantic, jazz) made strange, and little-known styles (e.g., atonal, minimalist) made familiar. How? By their juxtapositions, by changes between and in them.

The materials, selected first, determined the interactions. There are more instruments (piano, violin, and cello) and more to hear than in "Renascence."

In just one section, I heard the drone of the strings (minimalist) over (Romantic) runs up and down the keyboard, over syncopated (jazz) rhythms. The instruments switch, the strings play the tune, play the drone (two notes repeated, repeated, repeated).

The effect of the piece is that of listening to someone who speaks in your own language, but who interposes it, interweaves it, with other tongues. Your ear is surprised, then seduced, by the increasing familiarity of the strangeness and listens ever more carefully. This is how the familiar becomes strange, and the strange becomes more and more familiar.

Are there differences? Yes. In the compositions I picked, starting with form led to a leaner piece (quite like a contour drawing in which the outline implies the volume) where the organizing intelligence is primary. Starting with materials led to a lusher piece (more like a fully modeled, lavishly colored drawing) in which the sensory is salient.

Are there similarities? Yes, both are surprising to the ear, yet—like Berg—both provide a scaffolding of the familiar–enough to allow us to "hear" the novelty.

WHAT HAVE WE LEARNED?

Do constraints structure the creativity problem in music? Yes—and yes, I know you've heard this theme before. The variation on it here is that the *task constraints* (melody, harmony, rhythm) are the same ones that turn sounds (consonant or dissonant, tonal or atonal) into music.

How far? As always, it depends on the *goal constraint* of the composer. Structuring dissonance (Debussy, Stravinsky, Schoenberg) via novel *task constraints* was a goal that, once reached, completely changed the way sounds are put together, played, sung, heard.

This is influence on a grand scale. Less grand, but generative, is quotation, variation on borrowed themes (Bartok, Kodaly, Ives, Copland). The themes themselves are *subject constraints,* transformed according to the goal constraint of the borrower.

Finally, we have seen how one contemporary composer (Kramer) contrasts constraints to generate music that sounds surprisingly both new and known.

CHAPTER 9

Constraints for Developing Creativity

What else can we learn from Monet? What else can we learn from Picasso? What else can we learn from Matisse?

Instead of specifying constraints that structured the creativity problem in different domains, our question in this chapter is more general. What constraints help develop creativity in any domain? The answer is, basically, the same four for beginners of all ages. Since most beginners are children, let's talk a little about childhood.

Can you remember any pictures you made for Mom to hang on the refrigerator door? How about the one with the blue (for sky) strip across the top and the quarter of a yellow sun in one corner? It was a very cheery picture, with bright colors, happy sunshine. Didn't it have flowers lined up along a green (for grass) strip along the bottom? Sure.

How did I know about your picture? I drew it too. So did my daughter, and so did my nephew. After he had colored in the sky and the sun and the grass and the house and the tree, six-year old Michael said, "I didn't leave room for the dock." We taped on another piece of paper and Michael added the water, the dock, and two fish.

I copied Michael's picture so you could see that dock (Figure 9.1). Take a good look at it. It's drawn from above, instead of head-on (like the house and the tree and the sun)—different points of view in one painting. Isn't

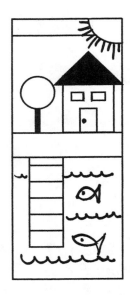

FIGURE 9.1. Conceptual perspective drawing of house and dock.

that what Braque and Picasso were doing? Yes, and for a surprisingly simi-lar reason. Braque and Picasso were painting what they knew, not what they saw. So was Michael.

The difference is that, for six-year olds, this is a developmental stage in learning to draw realistically. It's called conceptual perspective, which means that the viewpoint (the perspective) presents what the child knows about something. What six-year olds know are concepts, associative net-works for things in memory.

If Michael's associative network for "dock" looks like the diagram in Figure 9.2, the only way to show that a dock is a dock is to look straight down on it. How else could you see that all the boards are lined up with the water around them?

If this is a developmental stage, we can't say that Michael is creative. In fact, if he keeps drawing, he'll abandon his version of Cubism for the next stage, which is called perceptual (for what you perceive or see) perspective. The dock will be foreshortened and seen from the same point of view as the house and the flowers. The sky will reach down to the grass and the sun will probably not sit in the corner.

All children pass through these stages. This includes the gifted, who rush through the stages faster, and the prodigies, who rush past the gifted

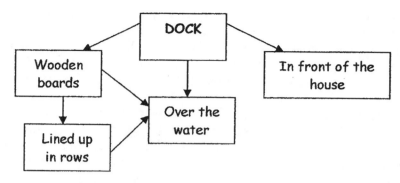

FIGURE 9.2. Associative network for dock.

to perform at adult levels before they're adults (Milbraith, 1998). What we call gifts are proclivities of importance in particular domains. Domains are areas of expertise with clearly defined performance standards and levels of mastery, along with methodologies for skill acquisition. A gift (like perfect pitch, Stravinsky's musical memory, Rothko's color memory) allows a child early entry into, and earlier mastery of, a particular domain. However, even with early entry, mastery takes about ten years.

What all this means is that while children can make things that are new and even generative, no beginner can change a domain. Early apprenticeships—Picasso's scribblings, Mozart's fingerings—don't alter art or music. What those efforts do is help beginners attain the expertise and high variability levels necessary for their later efforts to be influential. (I'll spell out what high variability levels are in the next section.)

CONSTRAINTS: CHILDREN TO CREATORS

There are four constraints on the path from child to creator. Three occur early; the fourth only appears with mastery.

The Domain Constraint

The initial constraint—the choice of domain or area of knowledge—is usually self-selected. Once chosen, the choice precludes other domains, promoting immersion and effort in the chosen area.

The choice itself results from an intense interest in something. Almost anything, chess or Pokemon, the piano or finger paint, can serve as the "something." Following the choice, the child acquires some elementary sort of expertise that's special (noticed, praised) because others (especially siblings or parents) don't have it. The five-year old son of a colleague once spent an entire afternoon at our lake house, not swimming, but drawing Pokemon characters and explaining their powers to the grown-ups who didn't know what he knew.

Children gifted in music or art or mathematics develop obsessive interests in their talent areas (Winner, 1996). Those not so specifically gifted will opt for activities that give each one an edge in the continuing competition for attention by peers, parents, and teachers. A girl recognized for her ability to jump double-dutch rope may well choose gymnastics. A boy whose dinosaur—or Pokemon—knowledge is admired could become hooked on biology or paleontology. A well-known painter said he became a painter because (while his addition homework never earned extra attention) his teachers always said that he drew better than anyone else in his grade. In the kindergarten class of the art director whose work we looked at earlier there were two bulletin boards—one for Ivan, the class artist, and one for everyone else. Expertise is always admired, even when it's elementary.

The Variability Constraint

There is something else to be learned, and learned early, by potential creators. Psychological studies (Stokes, 1999) show that when someone initially acquires a skill repertoire, he or she also learns how differently to use or apply the new skills. It's what I've called a *habitual variability level*—habitual because it's how differently someone *usually* performs in a particular area. I think of the level as a comfort range. I feel comfortable doing some things the same way, some in different ways, some in lots of different ways.

Think about something you like to do. (Yes, we did something like this earlier. Repeating helps remembering.) Now imagine a situation where the variability requirements for what you like doing are *subjectively* too high. How about painting three trees 20 different ways? How does that make you feel? A little anxious? Okay, just change the requirements so they're *subjectively* too low. Paint those trees exactly the same way 20 times. Feeling bored? Either way, anxious or bored, you'll be motivated to regain your habitual, comfortable level of variability (Stokes, 1995).

Highly creative individuals are comfortable being highly variable. Otherwise, they wouldn't (like the artists, architects, and others we've read about) continue to change their work, their ways of working, and ultimately, their domains. The source for these levels are the high *variability constraints* that accompany early and accelerated mastery of a domain.

Variability constraints determine how differently something must be done—in the same ways, or in different ways. High variability constraints preclude the reliable and repetitive, and promote the less probable, novel response. Accelerated learning (honors or advanced placement classes, condensing two years of study into one, and so forth), which requires doing many different and new things, promotes mastery and high variability levels at the same time. Mastery has that very important consequence mentioned earlier—being recognized as being special. Being recognized as special or unique is particularly important to gifted children, who often drop out of a domain if it is not highly regarded and valued in their culture (Feldman & Goldsmith, 1991).

The Early Task Constraints

Task constraints, specific to the selected domain, involve materials and conventions concerning their use. Drawing materials include pens, pencils, brushes, papers, fabrics, lithographic stones. Conventions include contour, perspective, single and multiple. Poetic materials include words and writing equipment, pencil and paper, computer keyboard. Conventions include meter, rhyme scheme, genre—epic, lyric, haiku.

Early exposure to *task constraints* has two special qualities. First, it's playful. Second, all attempts, approximations or successes, are attended to and encouraged. Play and attention are rewards. We can think of them as engines behind the child's seemingly effortless accomplishments. Teachers are warm, enthusiastic, ready to reward involvement rather than requiring systematic skill acquisition and application. Almost effortlessly, basic skills, the bases for more rigorous development, are acquired. In the process, the child also learns that persistence and industriousness, requirements in the next phase of the apprenticeship, are rewarded and rewarding.

During that next phase, precision takes precedence over playfulness. In drawing, this happens on the child's own initiative. At about eight or nine years of age children become concerned with accuracy and technical competence (Gardner, 1980). We all miss the spontaneity and naïve charm of the earlier production, but the child is correct in concentrating on correctness in technique. Until a pianist has all aspects of performance in perfect control, expressiveness is impossible (Sloboda, 1996). Until a painter has all aspects of rendering in hand, distortion is accidental rather than intentional.

Teachers now reserve reward for reaching successive levels of excellence. Constructive criticism replaces unconditional praise. Respect becomes as important as affection. Professional praise is now worth more than that of parents. This is the stage of "deliberate practice" (Ericcson, 1996, p. 21), which involves concentration, repetition, and correction of errors in a well-defined task with an appropriate level of difficulty.

The Later Goal Constraints

Once mastery is reached, the path diverges. One fork leads to the reliability of the expert; the other, to the unpredictability of the creator. For the latter, influential creativity depends on the specification and realization of novel goal constraints that expand his or her domain.

Since most of the book has focused on adult accomplishments, it's appropriate here to apply our constraint path to the early apprenticeships of two creators—as well as at the later, equally accelerated, one of a third.

EARLY APPRENTICES . . .

Gifted children are speedy, greedy skill acquirers. For them, accelerated, domain-specific training is critical. Acceleration makes high variability possible, expected, normative. By precluding repetition, it promotes and rewards high variability early in learning, when habitual levels in a domain are established. Domain-specificity leads to mastery, which the gifted child delights in employing and displaying. This delight has two sources: the intrinsic reward of skill development itself; and the extrinsic rewards of attention and praise paid to the work and to the highly variable way of working (Stokes, 2001).

Both speed and delight were evident in the young Claude Monet, who recalled filling the margins of his schoolbooks with garlands and "fantastical ornaments, which included highly irreverent drawings of my masters . . . with maximum distortion" (Wildenstein, 1996, p. 12). His drawings were regularly displayed and distributed to classmates. A sketch book from 1957, when Claude was 16, demonstrates his competence in traditional landscape techniques—composition, contour, shading, simplification—as well as exaggeration and condensation, the caricaturist's skills he acquired copying cartoons from newspapers. Monet's painting apprenticeship began the next year. His first master was Boudin, whose bright and sketchy beach scenes were shown in the framer's shop that also displayed and sold Monet's caricatures. The brightness and the sketchiness resulted from Boudin's practice—which became Monet's—of working rapidly, directly, *en plein air* in preference to the studio.

We can sketch a similar scenario for the young Pablo Picasso, whose later protean shifts in style and media have precursors in the rapid pace at which he (the prototypical gifted child) obsessively worked his way through the history of representational painting. Picasso's father, also a painter, introduced Pablo both to the traditional repertoire and to several unorthodox ways of working. Along with pencils, paints, and brushes, Pablo wielded scissors, paste, and pins. To amuse his sister and cousins, he cut out animals, garlands, and groups of figures with his aunt's embroidery shears. Like Monet, he drew cartoons. Formal study—and the first truly proficient drawings (of plaster casts)—began when Picasso was 11 (Richardson, 1991). In all, the pre-teen works are competent at, but not above, the level seen in gifted children today, all of whom proceed at relatively fast paces through the same developmental drawing stages.

. . . AND A LATE BLOOMER

Most gifted children choose the domain of their gift. Some creators choose their domains—and start their apprenticeships—well after childhood. My favorite art example is Henri Matisse, whose first paintbrush came in a kit his mother bought to amuse him while he was recovering from appendicitis in 1890 (Elderfield, 1992).

Like Monet and Picasso, Matisse's first paintings were copies—in his case, of the pictures that came with his paint set. At the time, he was 20 years old, with a law degree and a job as a legal clerk.

That paintbox opened for him, Matisse said, a kind of paradise. By 1891, he was in Paris starting his apprenticeship with the traditional (copying plaster casts at the Ecole des Beaux-Arts and paintings at the Louvre, oil painting with Moreau, studying perspective and geometry at the Ecole des Beaux-Arts Decoratifs) before mastering the contemporary (the color contrasts of Neo-Impressionism, the simplified forms of Cezanne, and sculpture). It is not until 1905 that the Fauve paintings which are recognizably Matisse's appear.

The example of Matisse shows that successful apprenticeships, which involve mastering the task constraints that define a domain, can start earlier or later, depending on when an intense interest is identified. Earlier or later, the same series of constraints are involved.

A CAVEAT: THE DANGER OF DILETTANTISM

Not every child is going to grow into a Claude Monet or a Henri Matisse, but each can have the pleasure of becoming an early expert, and a highly variable one, in something. If that something changes—and many times it will—the child who has experienced pleasure in persistence and reward for variability will apply himself industriously and variably to the challenge, the fun, of becoming an expert all over again.

Unfortunately, many bright and talented children are in danger of becoming dilettantes rather than experts. If Amy isn't obviously gifted in something, she'll be signed up for lots of things: a little piano, some soccer, certainly ballet. Amy will be well-rounded, but she won't experience the exhilaration of early expertise or the highs of variability. She'll also bore more easily, since each of her repertoires will be limited. To counter boredom, she'll change *what* she's doing rather than changing *the way* she's doing it. Creativity depends on changing the way you're doing something.

This isn't meant to suggest that children should be limited to one activity. But when they become interested, intensely, in one, that interest should be encouraged, supported, sustained. Growing up with several same-age cousins, all boys, I spent a lot of my free time bike riding and ball playing; I spent more of it by myself with a pencil or crayon in my hand. My parents sent me to Pratt's Saturday Art School for children. I designed and cut out clothes for paper dolls, decorated bulletin boards and windows in grade school. I started to take oil painting classes when I was 11. What I liked to do best was what I did better than anyone else.

By the way, adult beginners also run the risk of becoming dilettantes. Adult education is a booming business at universities and retirement communities. There's nothing wrong with sampling among domains, but when you find one that captivates you, concentrate on it. Choose classes that expand your first chorus, increase your skills, challenge and change your ways of looking, thinking, working.

A CONVERSATION: THE DANGER OF BOREDOM

Boredom can be beneficial if you have a high variability level and well-developed skills in a domain. The high variability level will motivate you to do things differently, and the wide skill repertoire will let you. However, boredom can be dangerous if you're a gifted child in a school where regular classes aren't challenging, and gifted classes are minimal.

I asked the gifted child I know best about this. He's another nephew, Ignazio Ciresi (personal interview, July 12, 2001). We call him Iggy. Iggy's gifts are mathematical and verbal. Ellen Winner (1996) identifies gifted children by the particular kinds of information they can easily hold in working memory. The mathematically gifted effortlessly retain numerical, spatial, and visual information. This obviously spills over into science, architecture, and design. The verbally gifted retain words.

Iggy's gifts were readily apparent in two very early interests—abstract art and ichthyology. At the stage when his brothers (Michael is his younger brother) were painting blue lines for sky and green ones for grass, Iggy was experimenting with what he called designs. His designs were abstract and very sophisticated. Some of them looked like Howard Hodgkin's paintings. Iggy's attention span for art is also extraordinary. We've gone to museums to study Ellsworth Kelly's shapes, or sit in front Jackson Pollack's drips (to figure out how they were done).

When he was in 5th grade, I helped Iggy illustrate a book he was writing about using different kinds of lures to catch different kinds of fish. To help me, he brought over a beautifully illustrated and highly technical fish encyclopedia. I asked if he knew everything in it. His answer was very matter-of-fact. "Not yet." More recently, he explained how to tell the mouth structure of a pike from that of a muskee, two fish from the same family that are found in our lake.

I asked Iggy, who was 13 and going into 8th grade, if we could talk about regular and gifted classes, which in his school district are the enrichment or pull-out variety. Pull-out means that children (chosen by teachers and/or tests) are pulled out of their regular classes for an hour to a day each week. What I'd like you to notice in our conversation are the italicized words. They point out Iggy's satisfactions and dissatisfactions, both related to his need for acceleration and challenge in the domains of his gifts. Our conversation went something like this.

AUNT PAT: Do you like school?

IGGY: Yeah, it's all right. It's a place to see friends, *to learn a little bit.*

AUNT PAT: Meaning?

IGGY: *I'd like to be learning more.*

AUNT PAT: Have any teachers ever given you more to do?

IGGY: In elementary school, in 3rd grade, one teacher had me *write a book,* and the principal *set up a school newspaper* so I could be the editor and the chief writer.

AUNT PAT: Anything else?

IGGY: In 5th grade, the math teacher had me *help other kids* with long division. You know, things like 460 divided by 20. I like helping other kids. I do that when we play basketball in the gym or outside too.

AUNT PAT: Do you coach?

IGGY: Not really, most of the kids know what to do, they just *don't get opportunities,* like having the ball fed to them.

AUNT PAT: What happened in middle school?

IGGY: In some classes, we're split up by ability. When that doesn't happen, the *teachers teach to the lowest level,* never to the highest. Last year, I was in the highest math, science, English, and social studies sections. Math and science are my best subjects. This year, I'll be in all the *honors sections*—algebra, literature, and geography.

AUNT PAT: You've been in the gifted program all along. How is it?

IGGY: Terrible.

AUNT PAT: I remember when you liked it.

IGGY: Well, now it's terrible. In the beginning (elementary school), it was fun. We were bused once a week to a different school for a whole day. We did projects like running a town (we collected taxes and apportioned them to projects and services) or picking a location (like the Arctic or upstate New York near Lake Ontario) and then figuring out how to survive there. The program's just *not gratifying anymore.*

AUNT PAT: What do you mean by less gratifying?

IGGY: Well, we get less time—only two periods a week—and it doesn't help me. We're going *back to slower stuff* (puzzles and drawing) *instead of going beyond* what we're learning now.

AUNT PAT: What would you like to go beyond to?

IGGY: *More challenging* math, astronomy, stuff like that. I'm looking forward to high school. There'll be *honors and AP classes,* and I'll be old enough to be a *research assistant* in ichthyology at the Museum of Natural History.

Fortunately for Iggy, his school has some accelerated honors classes and some extracurricular activities (football and baseball—he's on both teams) to which he can apply the concentrated attention and energy typical of the gifted. Acceleration (inside school) and interests (outside) compensate for the tedium of regular classes, and the boredom of a "slow" gifted program.

All this points to the potentially BIG problem. If tedium and boredom are *all* that's associated with school, gifted children can easily develop an aversion, an active dislike for school, an avoidance of learning. If that happens, they'll be handicapped in developing their gifts.

WHAT HAVE WE LEARNED?

Do constraints help creativity develop? Yes, and although we've concentrated on the development of gifted and talented children, the process is the same for all beginners.

It's important to remember, though, that all the process can do is *prepare* for creativity. Most of the prodigies, the gifted, the not-so-specifically gifted, and the late-bloomers, will become productive, if not prolific, in their areas of expertise. Many will produce novelties that are useful or generative. A few, a very few, will change their domains. Knowing how constraints help creativity develop can help keep all those options open.

CHAPTER 10

Central Concepts: A Recap

What did we learn from Monet? What did we learn from Wright? What did we learn from Debussy? What did we learn from Klee? What did we learn from Kundera? What did we learn from Aalto? What did we learn fromStravinsky?

WHAT DID WE LEARN?

Everyone who reads this book should learn some of the same things, but also some different things. The same things, hopefully, will be how constraints are used as creative tools; the different, examples of particular interest or usefulness to an individual reader. So, a summing–up of some important "same" things.

THE CREATIVITY PROBLEM

The creativity problem is *strategic* and *structural*. For the creator, it involves goal-directed specifying of paired constraints. One precludes (or limits search among) familiar, reliable responses; the other promotes (or directs search to) novel, surprising ones. The specification process structures the problem space, producing a solution path that simultaneously defines and satisfies a novel goal criterion.

The specification also turns an initially ill-defined problem into a well-defined one. Since well-defined problems can be solved with little search and little variability, great creators (who have high habitual variability levels) proceed to preclude their newly realized goal criteria and promote further novelties. For the student (of the domain or of creativity), reconstructing a constraint path "re-creates" and illuminates the structure of its solution.

CONSTRAINTS FOR CREATIVITY

Constraints for creativity are most succinctly and completely defined as tools that come in *pairs* which are *hierarchically organized* and *specific to domains*.

Constraints Are Tools

Constraints help develop creativity in beginners and help experts structure and solve creativity problems. However, learning to choose and use constraints doesn't guarantee creativity. What it does do is clarify and direct the creative process.

Constraints Come in Pairs

Constraints for creativity preclude reliable, already-recognized responses, and they promote novel, surprising ones. What gets precluded and what gets promoted are quite specific. To show how light breaks up, Monet precluded dark-light contrasts and promoted contrasts between similarly valued hues. To depict the patterns produced by an event, Calvino precluded the linear narrative and promoted his new, circular, recursive network.

Constraints Are Organized Hierarchically

The most important constraints, located at the top of the hierarchy, are goal constraints. Subject and task constraints follow from them. Comparing compact versions of Monet's first and third set of constraints (see Figure 10.1) should make this quite clear.

Constraints Are Domain-Specific

Your domain, or area of expertise, provides you both with the things you can *work with* and the things you can *work against*. What you work with are your first choruses. What you work against are currently accepted goal criteria, standards for what a painting, a novel, a floor plan, should be.

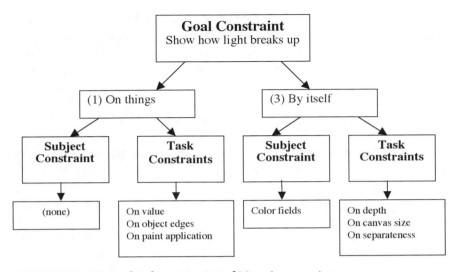

FIGURE 10.1. Hierarchical organization of Monet's constraints.

FIRST CHORUSES

Basic First Choruses

A succinct metaphor for a "basic" first chorus comes from the painter Paul Klee. One adapts oneself, he wrote, "to the contents of the paintbox" (Klee, 1879/1940). The contents are not just the paints, but all the ways that painters have used—and added to—the contents of the box. The paintbox, the basic first chorus, represents the skills and knowledge required for mastery of a domain. Once mastered, it becomes what you work with, the base from which you begin to improvise.

Different First Choruses

Of course, not every expert has the same first chorus. To the basics will be added *embellishments* and *emphases* in the domain, as well as contributions from *outside domains*. As the domain expands, succeeding generations will have larger first choruses both to master and to improvise on.

Embellishments

Regional embellishments contributed to the distinctive versions of modernism devised by Frank Lloyd Wright, Le Corbusier, and IM Pei. The open, horizontal orientation of the American prairie is reflected in Wright's organic architecture; the vertical enclosed Mediterranean village in Corbu's machine for living; the traditional Shinto shrine in Pei's Miho Museum.

Emphases

A selective emphasis on harmonic or rhythmic structure produced two different solutions to the same musical problem, ambiguity. Debussy's harmonic path is clearly related to his interests in early Church modes and Far Eastern scales; Stravinsky's percussive solution, to his youthful immersion in Russian rhythmic patterns and rituals. Virginia Woolf's memoirs concentrate on the current moment and emphasize the mimetic, the descriptive. William Styron's recurrent themes rely on patterns, repetitions that mirror the recurrences.

Outside Domains

Chemistry, an unlikely first chorus for painting, added Chevreul's color wheel to Monet's first chorus. The result was his novel goal: showing how light breaks up. A more closely related domain, decoration, contributed to Cubism. Braque's experience as a wallpaper hanger led to the insertion of *papiers colles,* pasted papers, in Cubist compositions. Musical expertise is critical to the multi-themed, polyphonic structure of Kundera's novels.

Succeeding Generations

Finally, each new generation starts with a larger first chorus than its predecessors. Aalto, having Corbu in his first chorus, could felicitously combine Mediterranean modernism with selective emphasis on the naturalism of his native North. Kawakubo and Rykiel, with Chanel and Schiaparelli in their first choruses, continuously surprise by combining the classic and the fantastic, along with references to their respective Japanese and French backgrounds.

Of course, once their basic skills have been acquired, the question that worries every new generation (faced with the creative achievements in its first chorus) is: *What is there left to do?* The answer always involves novel goal constraints.

GOAL CONSTRAINTS: WHAT'S LEFT TO BE DONE?

Only one thing can be done—*work against* a domain's and an individual's currently successful solutions.

Monet, again, shows how promoting the novel starts with precluding the reliable in what the individual himself does. What Monet did was continuously clarify his goal constraint (show how light breaks up) via a series of shifting sub-goals (on things, between things, alone) and the changes in subject and task constraints required to realize each in turn. The final goal constraint—and the final paintings—could not have been predicted from the first. The same incremental process appears in Matisse and Rothko. The early Fauve paintings do not forecast Matisse's late realization of "pure color and pure line" in cut and pasted papers. Rothko's early Surrealist style is unrelated to his late and luminous color fields.

It all starts with a novel goal constraint, but not necessarily with one individual.

Braque and Picasso together developed Cubism. Initially working against domain criteria (a single point of view in painting, paint what you see), they then worked against their own successive approximations (hermetic, synthetic, collage) to novel criteria (multiple points of view, paint what you know). The Pop Art movement of the 1960s began as a reaction against Abstract Expressionism. At that point in time, being noticed precluded belonging to the second generation of Abstract Expressionists. It promoted a set of goal criteria that were opposite to those of the first generation. Abstract Expressionism was painterly, emotional, hot. Pop had to be graphic, detached, cool. Subject and task constraints followed: Lichtenstein's comic–style drawings in day-glo colors, Rosenquist's collaged billboards, Warhol's replications and duplications.

The concluding (and comforting) thing to be said about novel goal constraints is that no one has to devise one alone. There are always external sources to work against (like Abstract Expressionism) or with (like Chevreul's color chart, or the Pop group).

LAST WORDS ON LATE BLOOMERS

Since I'm a late bloomer in psychology, I'd like to make one last connection—between creators and re-creating (or starting over). Creators have high habitual variability levels. They're comfortable with being very variable. They like trying new things; they dislike repeating old things. They preclude old solutions to promote novel ones. They never stop developing.

The connection comes here. *Development begins when an individual begins.* Matisse began to study painting in his 20s, Kandinsky in his 30s. Both practiced law before beginning again. Grandma Moses began in her 70s.

Not only can late bloomers become experts in new domains, they have a very good chance of becoming experts who are comfortable being very variable (and using constraints to stay that way). Why? First, there's always urgency in catching up. Fast-paced skill acquisition involves doing many different things and doing more difficult ones sooner rather than later. Different and difficult serve as constraints that preclude low and promote high variability. Second, late bloomers have repertoires from outside domains (like Braque's paper hanging and my advertising) that serve as supplemental first choruses in their new domains of expertise.[1]

It's never too late to pose a new creativity problem.

---

[1]For a related way of thinking about this, see Mumford and Gustafson (1988), who wrote that mid-life career changes spur creativity by "trigger[ing] the same integration of knowledge structures that characterizes young adults' major contributions" (p. 39).

References

CHAPTER 1
THE CREATIVITY PROBLEM

Austin, J. H. (2003). *Chase, chance, and creativity: The lucky art of novelty.* Cambridge, MA: MIT Press.

Csikszentmihalyi, M. (1996). *Creativity: Flow and the psychology of invention.* New York: HarperCollins.

Cooper, D. (1971). *The Cubist epoch.* New York: Praeger.

Newell, A., & Simon, H. A. (1972). *Human problem solving.* Englewood Cliffs, NJ: Prentice-Hall.

Reitman, E. (1965). *Cognition and thought.* New York: Wiley.

Rubin, W. (1989). *Picasso and Braque: Pioneering Cubism.* New York: Museum of Modern Art, Bullfinch Press; Boston: Little, Brown.

Simon, H. A. (1973). The structure of ill-structured problems. *Artificial Intelligence, 4,* 181–201.

Simonton, D. K. (1999). *Origins of genius: Darwinian perspectives on creativity.* New York: Oxford University Press.

Voss, J. F., & Post, T. A. (1988). On the solving of ill-structured problems. In M. T. H. Chi, R. Glaser, & M. J. Farr (Eds.), *The nature of expertise* (pp. 261–285). Hillsdale, NJ: Erlbaum.

CHAPTER 2
CONSTRAINTS AND FIRST CHORUSES

Abuhamdeh, S., & Csikszentmihalyi, M. (2004). The artistic personality: A systems perspective. In R. J. Sternberg, E. L. Grigorenko, & J. L. Singer (Eds.), *Creativity: From potential to realization* (pp. 31–42). Washington, DC: American Psychological Association.

Ericcson, K. A. (1996). The acquisition of expert performance: An introduction to some of the issues. In K. A. Ericcson (Ed.), *The road to excellence: The acquisition of expert performance in the arts and sciences, sports and games* (pp. 1–50). Mahwah, NJ: Erlbaum.

Holman, J., Goetz, E., & Baer, D. (1977). The training of creativity as an operant and an examination of its generalization characteristics. In B. C. Etzel, J. M. LeBlanc, & D. Baer (Eds.), *New developments in behavioral research: Theory, method, and application* (pp. 441–471). New York: Wiley.

Rivers, L. (1987, March 31). *Improvisation and the creative process in jazz and the visual arts.* Presentation given at Barnard College, Columbia University, NY.

Sloboda, J. (1996). The acquisition of musical performance: Deconstructing the "talent" account of individual differences in musical expressivity. In K. A. Ericcson (Ed.), *The road to excellence: The acquisition of expert performance in the arts and sciences, sports and games* (pp. 107–126). Mahwah, NJ: Erlbaum.

Stokes, P. D. (1995). Teaching variability in problem solving. In R. Kelder (Ed.), *Theories of learning: Teaching for understanding and creativity* (pp. 1–8). New Paltz, New York: SUNY.

Stokes, P. D. (1999a). Novelty. In M. A. Runco & S. R. Pritzker (Eds.), *Encyclopedia of creativity* (Vol. 2, pp. 297–304). New York: Academic Press.

Stokes, P. D. (1999b). Learned variability levels: Implications for creativity. *Creativity Research Journal, 12,* 37–45.

Stokes, P. D. (2001a). Variability, constraints and creativity: Shedding light on Claude Monet. *American Psychologist, 56,* 355–359.

Stokes. P. D. (2001b). Constraints and creativity: Experiments in psychology and art. In S. Nagel (Ed.), *Handbook of policy creativity* (pp. 33–48). Huntington, New York: Nova Science.

Stokes, P. D., & Fisher, D. (2005). Selection, constraints, and creativity case studies: Max Bickmann and Philip Guston. *Creativity Research Journal, 17,* 283–291.

Stokes, P. D., & Harrison, H. (2003). Constraints have different concurrent effects and aftereffects on variability. *Journal of Experimental Psychology: General, 131,* 552–566.

Winner, E. (1996). *Gifted children: Myths and realities.* New York: Basic Books.

CHAPTER 3
CONSTRAINTS FOR CREATIVITY IN LITERATURE

Byatt, A. S. (1992). *Sugar and other stories.* New York: Vintage.

Byatt, A. S. (1993). *Passions of the mind.* New York: Vintage.

Calasso, R. (1994). *The marriage of Cadmus and Harmony* (Tim Parks, Trans.). New York: Vintage.

Calvino, I. (1986). *The uses of literature* (Patrick Creagh, Trans.). New York: Harcourt Brace.

Calvino, I. (1992). *Invisible cities* (William Weaver, Trans.). New York: Harcourt Brace.

Calvino, I. (1993). *Six memos for the next millenium.* New York: Vintage International.

Dillard, A. (1982). *Living by fiction.* New York: Harper & Row.

Dillard, A. (1990). An American childhood. In *Three by Annie Dillard* (pp. 261–542). New York: Harper & Row.

Grescoe, P. (2001, June 27). Personal communication to the author.

Kundera, M. (1988). *The art of the novel* (Linda Asher, Trans.). New York: Harper & Row.

Kundera, M. (1996). *Slowness* (Linda Asher, Trans.). New York: HarperCollins.

McClelland, J. L. (2000). Connectionist models of memory. In E. Tulving & F. I. M. Craik (Eds.), *The Oxford handbook of memory* (pp. 583–596). New York: Oxford University Press.

McClelland, J. L., & Rummelhart, D. E. (1986). A distributed model of human learning and memory. In D. E. Rummelhart, J. L. McClelland, & the PDP Research Group (Eds.), *Parallel distributed processing: Explorations in the microstructure of cognition, Vol. I: Psychological and biological models* (pp. 170–215). Cambridge, MA: MIT Press.

Proust, M. (1982). *Remembrance of things past, Volumes I, II, III.* New York: Vintage Books. (Original work published 1871).

Shank, R. (1990). *Tell me a story: A new look at real and artificial intelligence.* New York: Charles Scribner's Sons.

Styron, W. (1993). *A tidewater morning.* New York: Vintage.

Tolstoi, L. (2003). *Anna Karenina.* New York: Barnes & Noble.

Woolf, A. (1976). *Moments of being.* New York: Harcourt Brace Jovanovich. (Original work published 1940).

CHAPTER 4
CONSTRAINTS FOR CREATIVITY IN ART

Anfam, D., & Mancusi-Ungaro, C. (1997). *Mark Rothko: The chapel commission.* Houston, TX: Menil Foundation.

Ashton, D. (1998). Mark Rothko and Abstract Expresionism. In *Mark Rothko, a special edition of Connaissance des Arts* (pp. 10–35).

Bonnard-Rothko: Color and light. (1997). Exhibition catalogue. New York: Pace-Wildenstein.

Castelman, Riva. (1986). *Jasper Johns: A print retrospective.* New York: Museum of Modern Art.

Chave, A. C. (1989). *Mark Rothko: Subjects in abstraction*. New Haven, CT: Yale University Press.

Cowart, J., Flam, J. D., Fourcade, D., & Neff, J. H. (Eds.). (1971). *Henri Matisse: Paper cut-outs*. New York: Henry N. Abrams.

Elderfield, J. (1976). *The "Wild Beasts": Fauvism and its affinities*. New York: Museum of Modern Art.

Flam, J. (Ed.). (1995). *Matisse on art*. Berkeley: University of California Press.

Forge, A. (1995). *Monet*. Chicago: Art Institute of Chicago.

Kimmelman, M. (2000, April 14). Unwavering scrutiny of being within the skin. *New York Times*, p. E 43.

Leymarie, J. (1955). *Fauvism*. Paris: Skira.

Morgan, G. (Ed.). (1996). *Monet: the artist speaks*. San Francisco: Collins Publishers.

Nodelman, S. (1998). The Rothko chapel paintings. In *Mark Rothko, a special edition of Connaissance des Arts* numéro hors série (pp. 10–35). Paris, Fondation Bayeler.

Patin, S. (1993). *Monet: The ultimate impressionist*. New York: Harry N. Abrams.

Rewald, J. (1986). *Cezanne: A biography*. New York: Harry N. Abrams.

Rose, B. (1986). *Twentieth century American painting*. New York: Skira.

Russell, J. (1981). *The meanings of modern art*. New York: Museum of Modern Art and Harper & Row.

Russell, J. (1982). *Jennifer Bartlett: In the garden*. New York: Harry N. Abrams.

Schneider, P. (1984). *Matisse*. New York: Rizzoli.

Seitz, W. C. (1982). *Claude Monet*. New York: Harry N. Abrams.

Stokes, P. D. (2001). Variability, constraints, and creativity: Shedding light on Claude Monet. *American Psychologist, 56*, 355–359.

Tucker, P. H., Shackleford, G. T. M., & Stevens, M., Curators. (1998). *Monet in the 20th century*. Exhibition. Museum of Fine Arts, Boston. New Haven, CT and London, England: Yale University Press.

Waldman, D. (1978). *Mark Rothko, 1903–1970: A retrospective*. New York: Harry N. Abrams.

Watkins, N. (2001). The genesis of a decorative aesthetic. In *Beyond the Easel: Decorative painting by Bonnard, Vuillard, Denis, and Roussel, 1890–1930* (pp. 1–30). Exhibition Catalogue. Chicago: The Art Institute of Chicago.

Wildenstein, D. (1996a). *Monet or the triumph of Impressionism*. Cologne, Germany: Taschen.

Wildenstein, D. (1996b). *Monet: Catalogue raisonne*. Cologne, Germany: Taschen.

CHAPTER 5
CONSTRAINTS FOR CREATIVITY IN FASHION

Baudot, F. (1996). *Chanel*. New York: Universe.

Baudot, F. (1997). *Elsa Shiaparelli*. New York: Universe.

Baudot, F. (1999). *Fashion: The twentieth century*. New York: Universe.

Edelman. A. H. (1997). *The little black dress*. New York: Simon & Schuster.

Engelmeer, R., & Engelmeer, P. W. (1997). *Fashion in film*. New York: Prestel.

Ewing, E. (1985). *History of 20th century fashion*. (Revised by Alice Mackell, 1992). New York: Costume and Fashion Press.

Fox, P. (1995). *Star style: Hollywood legends as fashion icons*. Santa Monica, CA: Angel City Press.

Herzog, C. C., & Gaines, J. M. (1991). 'Puffed sleeves before tea-time': Joan Crawford, Adrian and women audiences. In C. Ghedhill (Ed.), *Stardom: Industry of desire* (pp. 74–91). New York: Rutledge.

Martin, R. (1987). *Fashion and surrealism*. New York: Rizzoli.

Mauries, P. (1998). *Sonia Rykiel*. New York: Universe/Vendome.

Mendes, V., & de la Haye, A. (1999). *20th century fashion*. New York: Thames & Hudson.

Peacock. J. (1993). *20th century fashion: The complete sourcebook*. New York: Thames & Hudson.

Riva, M. (1992). *Marlene Dietrich*. New York: Ballentine Books.

Russell, D. A. (1985). *Stage costume design: Theory, technique, and style*. Englewood Cliffs, NJ: Prentice-Hall.

Starr, J. (2001, June 29). Personal communication.

Steele, V. (1991). *Women of fashion: Twentieth century designers*. New York: Rizzoli.

Tapert, A. (1998). *The power of glamour: The women who defined the age of stardom*. New York: Crown.

CHAPTER 6
CONSTRAINTS FOR CREATIVITY IN ARCHITECTURE

Blake, P. (1965). *Frank Lloyd Wright: Architecture and space*. Baltimore: Penguin Books.

Blake, P. (1966). *Le Corbusier*. Baltimore: Penguin Books.

Curtis, W. J. R. (1996). *Modern architecture since 1900*. London: Phaidon.

Donzel, C. (1998). *New museums*. Paris: Telleri.

Kaczka, D. (2001, September 8). Personal communication.

Kaufman, E. Jr., & Raeburn, B. (Eds.). (1965). *Frank Lloyd Wright: Writings and buildings*. Cleveland, OH: World Publishing Company.

Le Corbusier (1986). *Toward a new architecture*. (Frederick Etchells, Trans.). New York: Dover Publications. (Original work published 1931.)

Newhouse, V. (1998). *Toward a new museum*. New York: Monacelli Press.

Richards, J. M. (1940). *An introduction to modern architecture*. Baltimore: Penguin Books.

Trencher, M. (1996). *The Alvar Aalto guide*. New York: Princeton Architectural Press.

Zaknic, I. (Ed.). (1987). Le Corbusier (1946–1970). *Journey to the east*. Cambridge, MA: MIT Press.

CHAPTER 7
CONSTRAINTS FOR CREATIVITY IN ADVERTISING

Higgins, D. (1965). *The art of writing advertising: Conversations with masters of the craft.* Chicago: NTC Business Books.

Kanner, B. (1999). *The 100 best TV commercials . . . and why they worked.* New York: Times Books.

Leichman, S. (2002, January 20). Personal communication.

Lorin, P. (2001). *Five giants of advertising.* New York: Assouline.

Millman, N. (1988). *Emperors of adland.* New York: Warner Books.

Polykoff, S. (1975). *Does she . . . or doesn't she? And how she did it.* Garden City, NY: Doubleday.

Reeves, R. (1961). *Reality in advertising.* New York: Knopf.

Sherman, I. (2002, January 26). Personal communicaton.

Twitchell, J. B. (2000). *Twenty ads that shook the world: The century's most groundbreaking advertising and how it changed us all.* New York: Crown.

Young, J. W. (1975). *A technique for producing ideas.* Chicago: NTC Business Books.

CHAPTER 8
CONSTRAINTS FOR CREATIVITY IN MUSIC

Bernstein, L. (1976). *The unanswered question: Six talks at Harvard.* Cambridge, MA: Harvard University Press.

Cone, E. T. (1979). *Roger Sessions on music: Collected essays.* Princeton, NJ: Princeton University Press.

Copland, A. (1953). *What to listen for in music.* New York: Mentor.

Copland, A., & Perlis, V. (1984). *Copland: 1900 through 1942.* New York: St. Martin's/Marek.

Fish, J. (Ed.). (1997). *Composers on music: Eight centuries of writing.* Boston, MA: Northeastern University Press.

Kramer, J. (2002, January 20). Personal communication.

Leibowitz, H. A. (Ed). (1969). *Musical impressions: Selections from Paul Rosenfeld's criticism.* New York: Hill and Wang.

Morgan, R. P. (1991). *Twentieth-century music: A history of musical style in modern Europe and America.* New York: Norton.

Nicols, R. (1972). *Debussy: Oxford studies of composers.* London: Oxford University Press.

Oliver, M. (1995). *Igor Stravinsky.* London: Phaidon.

Rich, A. (1995). *American pioneers: Ives to Cage and beyond.* London: Phaidon.

Schonberg, H. C. (1970). *The lives of the great composers.* New York: W. W. Norton.

Stravinsky, I., & Croft, R. (1962). *Stravinsky: Explorations and developments.* Garden City, NY: Doubleday.

Strein, L. (Ed.). (1975). *Style and idea: Selected writings of Arnold Schoenberg.* Berkeley: University of California Press.

Thompson, O. (1967). *Debusssy: Man and artist.* New York: Dover.

CHAPTER 9
CONSTRAINTS FOR DEVELOPING CREATIVITY

Elderfield, J. (1992). *Henri Matisse: A retrospective.* New York: Harry N. Abrams.

Ericcson, K. A. (1996). The acquisition of expert performance: An introduction to some of the issues. In K. A. Ericcson (Ed.), *The road to excellence: The acquisition of expert performance in the arts and sciences, sports, and games* (pp. 1–50). Mahwah, NJ: Erlbaum.

Feldman, D. H., & Goldsmith, L. (1991). *Nature's gambit: Child prodigies and the development of human potential.* New York: Columbia University, Teacher's College.

Gardner, H. (1980). *Artful scribbles: The significance of children's drawings.* New York: Basic Books.

Milbrath, C. (1998). *Patterns of artistic development in children: Comparative studies of talent.* New York: Cambridge University Press.

Richardson, J. (1991). *A life of Picasso: 1881–1906* (Vol. 1). New York: Random House.

Sloboda, J. A. (1996). The acquisition of musical performance expertise: Deconstructing the "talent" account of individual differences in musical expressivity. In K. A. Ericcson (Ed.), *The road to excellence: The acquisition of expert performance in the arts and sciences, sports, and games* (pp. 107–126). Mahwah, NJ: Erlbaum.

Stokes, P. D. (1995). Teaching variability in problem solving. In R. Kelder (Ed.), *Theories of learning: Teaching for understanding and creativity* (pp. 1–8). New Paltz, New York: SUNY.

Stokes, P. D. (1999). Learned variability levels: Implications for creativity. *Creativity Research Journal, 12,* 37–45).

Stokes, P. D. (2001). Variability, constraints, and creativity: Shedding light on Claude Monet. *American Psychologist, 56,* 355–359.

Wildenstein, D. (1996). *Monet or the triumph of Impressionism.* Cologne, Germany: Taschen

Winner, E. (1996). *Gifted children: Myths and realities.* New York: Basic Books.

Zimmerman, E. (1995). It was an incredible experience: The impact of education opportunities on a talented student's artistic development. In C. Golumb (Ed.), *The development of artistically gifted children: Selected case studies* (pp. 135–170). Hillsdale, NJ: Erlbaum.

CHAPTER 10
CENTRAL CONCEPTS: A RECAP

Klee, F. (Ed.). (1964). *The diaries of Paul Klee, 1898–1918*. Berkeley: University of California Press. (Original work published 1910.)

Mumford, M. D., & Gustafson, S. B. (1988). Creativity syndrome: Integration, application, and innovation. *Psychological Bulletin, 103*, 27–43.

APPENDIX A

"Working With Constraints" for Columbia University Students

Working With Constraints I: Learning to Write in a Different Voice[1]

What can we learn from writing in someone else's style? My students improvise on three "first choruses," experiment with a triad of literary voices. The form is memoir. They learn to identify and use constraints that generate more expressive, evocative snapshots of their own lives.

FIRST DRAFT: WRITING IN YOUR OWN VOICE

Students write a short (one page) memoir on one of the following themes:

- Write about the *first time* you did something—went to school, went to camp, rode a bike, gave a speech. Where were you? What were you wearing? Whom were you with? How did you feel?
- Write about a *repeated pattern* in your life. The pattern can involve how you act (arrange rooms, solve problems, choose friends) or how you feel.

Identifying Other Voices

Three authors discussed in chapter 3 have served as "first choruses" for a seminar I teach at Barnard. The three are A. S. Byatt, Italo Calvino, and

[1]Instructions given to students are bulleted.

Annie Dillard. The choice was based on two things. First, each had written about writing and about their writing. Second, each wrote in a *noticeably different style.*

Identifying Their Constraints

Before the fictions, the class reads essays about writing. Before "Sugar" they read "Passions of the Mind," in which Byatt discusses the way that metaphor serves as scaffolding for her fictions, how Browning taught her to tell and retell, make and remake a narrative. Before "Invisible Cities" they discuss "The Uses of Literature," where Calvino defines his "territory" as fantasy, the fantastically imagined, multiply-mirrored effects of extraordinary events. Prior to "An American Childhood comes "Living by Fiction," where Dillard delineates the differences between painterly prose, elaborate and alliterative, demanding attention for itself, and her more sparing, plainer prose, which modestly points to the world.

For each author in turn, students must do two things:

- Specify the constraints that generate each author's "voice" or style. For example, Byatt's include *mimesis* (description), *metaphor* (relationship), and *patterning* (structure).
- Match the constraints with examples (sentences, paragraphs) from the memoirs (for Byatt and Dillard) or novel (for Calvino).

SECOND DRAFT: THE FIRST AUTHOR'S VOICE

Students are now instructed to pick up someone else's pen and compose with their constraints in mind. For example, the instructions given for Byatt are:

- Look at the sentences you selected from Byatt. Think about the constraints they satisfied.
- Rewrite your memoir in Byatt's voice. This does not mean paraphrase yourself. It means *rethink, restructure, rewrite*. The new style may necessitate greater or lesser detail. It may require a different point (or several points) of view. You may need less or more structure, longer or shorter sentences, added or muted emotions.
- Read your second draft. Read it aloud.
- Does it work? Was Byatt's voice easy or difficult to adopt? Did you enjoy writing differently? Did the new voice with its clearly specified constraints facilitate saying what you wanted to convey? If so, in what ways?

- Was it impossible? Did it hinder what you wanted to say? If your answer is yes, try again with a different memory; Byatt's style may simply not serve for your initial snapshot. Write another first draft, write another second, reevaluate the results.

THIRD AND FOURTH DRAFTS: THE SECOND AND THIRD AUTHORS' VOICES

For Calvino and Dillard, students follow the directions given for the second draft.

Comparing the Constraints

Students reread all three revisions of their memoirs, answering the following questions.

- Which borrowed voice sounded best when you wrote in it?
- Which constraints were easiest to adopt? Why?
- Which best expressed what you wanted to say? Why?

FINAL DRAFT: BACK TO YOUR OWN VOICE

Students re-write their memoir in their own voices and compare it to their first draft, answering the following questions.

- Can you identify the constraints in each version?
- Have they become clear to you?
- Have they changed? In what ways? Why?

STUDENT REACTIONS

Students are very resistant to writing in someone else's style—<u>until</u> they try it, and discover the gifts a literary "first chorus" offers them. For example, one student said that using the constraints of a highly creative author enhanced her own writing for two reasons: first, it generated "highly focused work," and second, she was unable to "simply follow my typical train of thought." Another said that, <u>before</u> working with Calvino's constraints, there were things she had tried to express in words, but couldn't; "wanting what one cannot have" is how she put it. With the constraints, she could.

In addition to improving their writing skills, experiencing how another author's clearly identified constraints facilitated or hindered what they want to convey was critical to students' true comprehension of the strategic ways in which constraints (goal, subject, task) are chosen, and how specific constraints can help structure and solve the creativity problem (even at their level).

Working With Constraints II: Learning to Take Chances

What can we learn by copying or working like a famous artist? It's not to represent a particular painting, but to discover and practice using the constraints that made the work possible. It's not by chance that Jean Arp and Ellsworth Kelly are our teachers this time.

USING CHANCE AS A TASK CONSTRAINT

Artists have always used chance as a *task constraint* to introduce surprise into their work. The person meant to be surprised is the artist. The purpose is to preclude reliable solutions and promote novel ones to a creativity problem.

Accidents, being chance events, are always surprising. Some artists, like Leonardo da Vinci looking for patterns in puddles and stains, search for accidents. Others try to manufacture them. The Surrealists, for example, began paintings with "automatic writing," a kind of doodling designed to preclude control and promote chance.

In both cases, "accidents" are only meant to jump-start the creative process. Whether a composition is musical, poetic, or painterly, accident or chance is never the only constraint. The elements (doodles, words, colors, configurations, durations) chosen or arranged by chance procedures are subject to other constraints (*goal* and *task*).

FIXED ELEMENTS, CHANCE ARRANGEMENTS: ARP AND KELLY

Chance is a particularly appropriate constraint in making collages. Many of Jean Arp's collages were produced in three steps. The artist (1) chose colored papers or pictures to be (2) torn and tossed on the floor, and (3) re-arranged to satisfy his compositional criteria. The first two steps involved *task constraints* (selecting the set of elements, using chance to produce a provisional arrangement). In the third, *goal constraints* (like rhythm, depth, contrast, complexity) were invoked to produce the final arrangement.

Ellsworth Kelly's arrangements, organized by grids, are more formal than Arp's. Kelly begins with a drawing or small painting, cuts it into identical shapes (rectangles or squares), and arranges the shapes (strictly by chance) into a larger rectangle or square. Kelly also uses the grid format in painting directly, filling in the squares from a limited number of colors, choosing among them by chance as he proceeds.

Exercise 1: Arp's Constraints

To follow Arp's procedure, students have to choose a *goal constraint,* a criterion to help them select from, or rearrange, the chance configurations produced by tearing and tossing colored papers. The goal constraint also determines which colored papers one starts with, and the ways in which one cuts or tears them.

One goal used in this exercise demands a dynamic pattern with high contrast. The easy part is choosing the colors. For high contrast, good choices are black, white, and one primary hue, like red. The hard part is this: **While the goal is stated verbally, it can only be recognized visually.**

The following are the steps the students followed:

- **Cut** or **tear** the papers into hard-edged geometric shapes (squares, triangles, rectangles). The shapes can differ in size.
- **Place** three large sheets of white or tan paper on the floor.
- **Pick up** the shapes randomly. Drop one at a time onto the large sheets.
- **Compare** the three by-chance configurations. How well do they meet your initial *goal criteria* (dynamic, high contrast)? Is one more visually interesting than the other two? Why? Is there greater contrast among the color, shapes, and sizes of the cutouts? Is the balance more asymmetric? Is there a visual rhythm? [Notice how this part of the assignment helps clarify and articulate the criteria.]
- **Separate** the most interesting composition from the others. How well does it meet your more completely specified goal criteria? Would you change it?
- If yes, then **change** it.

Following my own directions, I came up with three collages (see Figure A.1).

The gray shapes were red in the originals. I chose the one on the left as best. Why? It had the clearest movement. The shapes seemed to be falling. The two black ones (triangle and rectangle) at the lower right visually pulled down the others. I didn't change it.

Exercise 2: Kelly's Constraints

In Kelly's collage procedure, the final arrangement is all-chance, no-choice. This makes it seem unnecessary to select a *goal criterion,* but you still have to. Some students could only articulate a criterion after several unsuccessful attempts to produce a satisfactory collage. The question they asked of an at–last satisfactory one was simple: "Why does it work?"

Here are the steps in the exercise.

- **Make** a rectangular drawing and an empty box the same size as the drawing.
- **Cut** the drawing into even strips. (I kept folding in half until I got 8 pieces).
- **Arrange** the pieces by chance in the empty box. (I turned the pieces upside down and tried to shuffle them. I picked them up in no particular order).
- **Paste** the pieces down. (No rearranging. This is not the Arp exercise).
- **Compare** the original and the re-composed drawings. How do they differ? Which is more interesting? Why?
- What is the **goal constraint?**

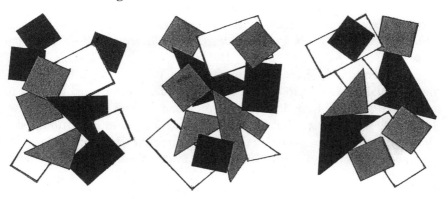

FIGURE A.1. Arp exercise collages.

FIGURE A.2. Kelly–exercise collage.

My best attempt started with a contour drawing (continuously drawn with all lines connected) of a eucalyptus branch. It's on the left in Figure A.2. On the right is the collage that was cut and rearranged by chance. I judged it moderately successful. Why? It retained the rhythm of the original, but in a surprising way.

STUDENT REACTIONS

The students said that "cut-and-paste" was like kindergarten, but a lot harder. They learned a lot doing these exercises Most important was realizing why *task constraints* (e.g., choosing the elements) follow from *goal constraints*.

To select colors, shapes, and, finally, one of their three Arp-like collages necessitated a criterion to choose each by. Students discovered too that to construct a "good" Kelly-like collage, they had to start with simple drawings. The ones that worked best were like Kelly's contour (outline only) drawings. Why? More complex drawings resulted in chaotic, too variable, rearrangements. (Think about Picasso and Braque's simplifying and enlarging their fractured Cubist shapes when their paintings became incomprehensible.) Simpler, connected ones produced rhythmic patterns that were not unlike the originals, just more surprising in their juxtaposition of parts.

APPENDIX B

"Working With Constraints" for a Group of Students at the School of the Art Institute of Chicago

Working With Constraints III: Learning to Chart Your Own Constraints

What can you learn about your own use of constraints? This set of questions is designed to help identify the constraints you've worked with, and how they've changed as your work developed. How many questions you can answer will depend on how long you've been working in your domain. If you can't answer them all, you can always come back. If you have all the answers, you should also come back periodically to consider what constraints could help you to continue developing.

CAN YOU IDENTIFY YOUR "FIRST CHORUSES"?

A first chorus is what you improvise on, make variations of. It's what you *work with*. One of your first choruses is your **domain** (1, 2, 3, or 4–dimensional design), and your **training** in that domain.

- What were the earliest *task constraints* (and the criteria for judging them) that you learned? If you're an artist, look at your beginner sketchbooks, your initial oil paintings or prints.
- Which task constraints do you still use? (My palette is the one I used in my first oil painting class at Pratt.)

Other first choruses are **particular artists** or **specific pieces** that "struck" you in some way, that let you "see" or "hear" differently, made you recognize possibilities that could be realized in slightly (or radically) different ways.

- Who and/or what influenced you **early on?** How?
- **Later on?** In what ways?

What Was the First Set of Constraints You Could Call Your Own?

- What was the **goal constraint** that caused the change?
- What **task constraints** did you adopt?
  What did they preclude?
  What did they promote?
- Were the constraints **generative?**
  Did they lead to different kinds of solutions to your problem?
  What solutions?
  Did they lead to new problems?
  What problems?

What Are Your Current Constraints?

- What is your current **goal constraint?** Try to be specific; "changing" or "doing something new or different" isn't helpful.
- What **task constraints** are you utilizing to realize it?
  What do they preclude?
  What do they promote?

How Did You Get From Your First Constraints to Your Current Constraints?

This is a very hard question. To answer it, you'll have to produce (in your mind's eye, via photos or real pieces) a **personal retrospective**, dividing your work into different stages (if you've worked long enough).

- What instigated the changes? Did a particular show (like Bonnard's colors changing Rothko's palette) or problem (like Debussy dealing with tonality) push the process?
- Can you list your own series of constraints? Be sure to include what they precluded and what they promoted.

WHAT'S NEXT?

Of course, you can't answer this question completely or even correctly (since you haven't done what's next, yet). What you can do is look for clues, like these:

- What are you currently **dissatisfied** with?

  This may not be clear yet; you may simply be **bored with** a reliable solution to the painting or sculpting problem at hand. Try to make your discontent specific.

  Alternatively, you could be **discomfited by** something new in your work that you haven't worked out yet. Nobody is comfortable with the novel. Put a too-new thing aside. Make it familiar by going back to it again and again.

  Treat dissatisfaction as a positive. It can help you identify what you want to *work against*.

- What are you currently **attracted** to?

  What you're attracted to is very important because a change in what attracts you (or repels you) is usually a signal that your work (particulary your goal constraint) is changing or going to change.

  Is there someone or some school (say 15th century Flemish, which influenced Bill Viola's very contemporary video, *Quintet of Remembrance*) whose work you weren't interested in before, but are today? What about it interests you? Try to relate your interest to your work in progress.

CONSTRAINTS IN RETROSPECT

Fill in the sample worksheet, following. You'll probably have to add pages. Try to break your work into stages separated by the constraints you used. Always think about your constraints in pairs. Note what each precluded and promoted.

When your work changes, add the constraints that accompany the changes. Use them as an opportunity to rethink the whole series, identifying new connections, noticing smaller changes that didn't seem important when you first made them.

STUDENT REACTIONS

The artist who had students in her studio classes fill out the worksheet (at home) to discuss in class said there were three notable results. First, all her students participated in the discussion. None had been so animated before. Second, students who had been resistant to her suggestions for experimentation in their work were "better able to act" when they "discovered" the necessity for change themselves. Third, "they could see how various degrees of confidence had reasons in their histories (i.e., skills they had acquired or not acquired), and that less confidence was not a student's fault, but was based on something that could be tackled." My friend's final comment was "All in all, a great success" (Adeheid Mers, personal communication, April 30, 2003).

WORKSHEET			
Goal (Sub-goals)	Subject	Task	Date

Index

Pioneers of Personality Science
Autobiographical Perspectives

Stephen Strack, PhD
Bill N. Kinder, PhD, Editors

The field of personology, or personality, is enjoying great growth, spurred by findings coming from behavior genetics, evolutionary psychology, rethinking of the Diagnostic and Statistical Manual for Mental Disorders definition of personality disorders, and advances in test construction and psychometrics.

Sixteen biographical chapters written by those who were the pioneers of personality assessment trace the development of the field. With accompanying photos and a concise bibliography from each contributor, this one-of-a-kind compilation of the history, present, and future of personology chronicles the following leaders:

- Jack Block • Arnold H. Buss • James N. Butcher • Richard Dana
- Leonard Handler • Robert R. Holt • Wayne Holtzman • Samuel Karson
- Paul M. Lerner • Jane Loevinger • Joseph Masling • Theodore Millon
- Edwin S. Shneidman • Norman Sundberg • Irving B. Weiner
- Marvin Zuckerman

Partial Contents:

- My Unexpected Life
- A Report on Myself: The Science and/or Art of Assessment
- A Psychologist Grows in Brooklyn: Reflections from the Past
- A Life-Long Attempt to Understand and Assess Personality
- Have PhD, Will Travel
- From Freud to Gehrig to Rapaport to DiMaggio
- Confessions of an Iconoclast: At Home on the Fringe
- A Blessed and Charmed Personal Odyssey
- The Shaping of Personality: Genes, Environments, and Chance Encounters

December 2005   440pp   0-8261-3205-7   hardcover

11 West 42nd Street, New York, NY 10036-8002 • Fax: 212-941-7842
Order Toll-Free: 877-687-7476 • Order On-line: www.springerpub.com

Psychodrama in the 21st Century
Clinical and Educational Applications

Jacob Gershoni, MSW, ACSW, TEP, Editor

"This contribution addresses the power, depth, breadth, and scope of Moreno's work."

—from the Foreword by **Robert W. Siroka**
PhD, TEP, CGP
Past President, American Society of Group
Psychotherapy and Psychodrama
Director, The Sociometric Institute

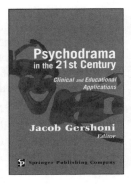

This book anthologizes a wide range of creative and innovative psychodrama applications in a variety of settings, offering numerous case examples. It covers the following subjects:

Partial Contents:

Part I: Psychodrama and Other Methods
- Psychoanalytic Group Psychotherapy, *Sandra Garfield*
- Bowen's Systems Theory, *Chris Farmer* and *Marcia Geller*
- Structural Family Therapy, Jacob Gershoni
- Art Therapy, *Jean Peterson*

Part II: Applications with various groups
- Psychodrama in Everyday Life, *Adam Blatner*
- Latency Age Children, *Mary Jo Amatruda*
- War Veterans, *Elaine Camerota* and *Jonathan Steinberg*
- Addictions and Women, *Tian Dayton*
- Gay and Lesbian Community, *Jacob Gershoni*
- Couples' Therapy, *Joseph Romance*

Part III: Application in Training and Consultation
- Experiential Education, *Herb Propper*
- Training Trial Lawyers, *James Leach*
- Consultations with Primary Care Physicians, *Chris Farmer*

2003   312pp   0-8261-2175-6   hardcover

11 West 42nd Street, New York, NY 10036-8002 • Fax: 212-941-7842
Order Toll-Free: 877-687-7476 • Order On-line: www.springerpub.com